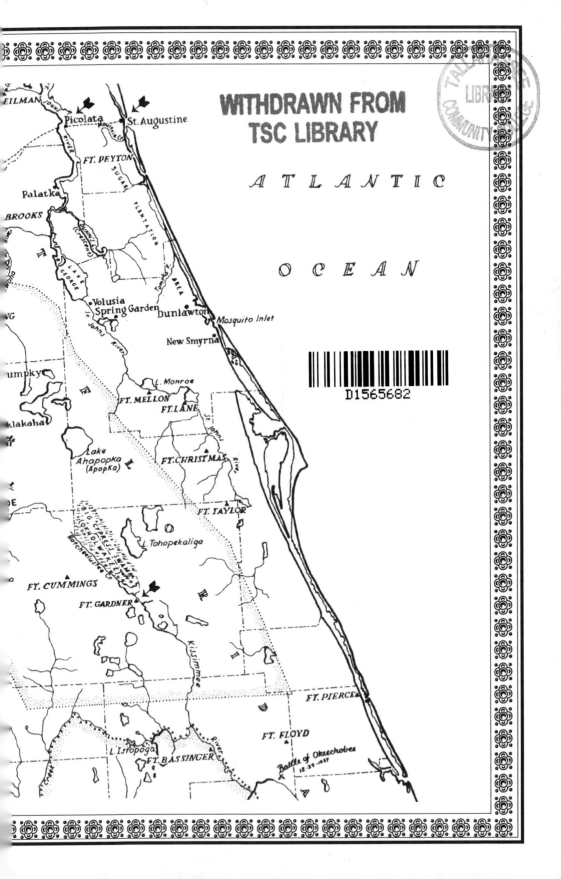

EILMAN

Picolata · St. Augustine

FT. PEYTON

Palatka

BROOKS

LAKE GEORGE

·Volusia
Spring Garden Dunlawton
Mosquito Inlet

New Smyrna

L. Monroe

FT. MELLON
FT. LANE

Lake
Ahapopka
(Apopka)

FT. CHRISTMAS

FT. TAYLOR

L. Tohopekaliga

FT. CUMMINGS

FT. GARDNER

Kissimmee River

FT. PIERCE

FT. FLOYD

L. Istopoga
FT. BASSINGER

Battle of Okeechobee
12-25-1837

ATLANTIC

OCEAN

D1565682

AMIDST A STORM OF BULLETS

Henry Prince

Amidst a Storm of Bullets

The Diary of Lt. Henry Prince in Florida
1836–1842

Edited by

Frank Laumer

Foreword by

John K. Mahon

Seminole Wars Historic Foundation Inc.
Contribution Number One

University of Tampa Press
Tampa, Florida
1998

Manufactured in the United States of America
First Edition

The University of Tampa Press
401 West Kennedy Boulevard
Tampa, Florida 33606

ISBN: 1-879852-59-4

On the dust jacket: *The Withlacoochee Abyss* by Jackson Walker. Oil on board. 48"x 40". 1992. Reproduced by permission of the artist.

Library of Congress Cataloging-in-Publication Data

Prince, Henry, 1811-1892.
  Amidst a storm of bullets : the diary of Lt. Henry Prince in Florida, 1836-1842 / edited by Frank Laumer.
  p. cm. — (Contribution / Seminole Wars Historic Foundation ; no. 1)
  ISBN 1-879852-59-4
  1. Seminole War, 2nd, 1835-1842—Personal narratives. 2. Prince, Henry, 1811-1892—Diaries. 3. United States. Army.—History Seminole War, 2nd, 1835-1842. I. Laumer, Frank. II. Title. III. Series: Contribution (Seminole Wars Historic Foundation) ; no. 1.
  E83.835 .P875 1998
  973.5'7—dc21
                                                                    98-40151
                                                                    CIP

THIS BOOK IS DEDICATED TO

THOSE WHO WERE THERE

CONTENTS

ILLUSTRATIONS

FOREWORD

Frank Laumer experienced a rare thrill, stemming from his study of the Second Seminole War (1835–1842), with the discovery of a diary kept during that war by Lt. Henry Prince. The manuscript had been out of sight in attic trunks for 142 years. Laumer brought the diary to the P. K. Yonge Library of Florida History at the University of Florida. Now, after twenty years of deciphering and researching, Laumer, with the help of many others, presents Prince's field notes in their entirety.

In the Introduction, Laumer traces Prince's life from birth until his graduation from the U.S. Military Academy in September 1835. Three months later 2nd Lt. Prince was on duty in Florida.

His diary, which begins on 10 January 1836, is the only one known to have been written by a participant during the Second Seminole War. It is not a reminiscence nor a rewritten journal, but a series of notes taken in the field day by day, here reproduced unaltered.

Prince's entries transport the reader back to the frontier Florida of the 1830s. Prince, who grew up in Maine, suffered from the weather and from certain characteristics of the peninsula. He recorded dispassionately the clouds of mosquitoes robbing men of their sleep and driving horses to distraction. Prince had to adjust and he did. For example, on 24 April 1837, he slogged four hours through a slough in pouring rain. Once across, however, he laid a blanket on the soaked ground, wrapped himself in his cloak, and slept, "as comfortable as a mud turtle."

Because Prince describes the weather, the reader can feel its relationship to military events. He includes many other details of significance: distances marched; distances between places; infantry companies serving mounted (presumably on Indian ponies); and the polyglot nature of the enlisted men of the United States Army. His is the only eyewitness account of the siege of Camp Izard, 28 February – 6 March 1836, a crucial action in the Seminole War. Prince was so skillful a mapmaker and freehand artist that archeologists, using his material, have been able to locate some wartime sites on today's ground; for example, Powell's (Osceola's) Town.

Beginning on 22 May 1837, Prince was in Cuba and Nassau on sick leave. He returned to Florida on 3 January 1838. By that time, the war had shifted from the area of the Withlacoochee River southward 150 miles to the Lake Okeechobee region. At one time or another, he visited all the major battlefields and wrote detailed descriptions of them. Absent from Florida on other duty during 1839, 1840, and 1841, he made only a few entries. The diary recommences in Florida on 5 April 1842, and continues for part of that month before he was transferred out of the Territory again.

Laumer did extensive and effective research in preparing the Epilogue. It tells the story of Prince's life from 1842 to the lonely tragedy of his death in London, aged 81. It is an elegant portion of writing.

–John K. Mahon
Emeritus Professor of History
University of Florida

PREFACE

My home is on the north bank of the Withlacoochee River, half a mile west of Fort Dade. Thirteen miles north by the Ft. King Road lies Dade Battlefield State Park. On the 29th of October, 1978, I received a telephone call from Winnie Murphy, Museum Guide at the Battlefield. A visiting couple claimed to own a diary written during the years 1836 through 1842 by an officer of the United States Army stationed in Florida during that period. The diary allegedly included maps, sketches of Seminole War forts, even a drawing of Dade Battlefield itself done only weeks after the battle. For fifteen years I had been doing research and writing on everything relating to this bloody engagement between Seminole Indians and American soldiers. I immediately invited the couple to visit me.

Mr. Ralph Coggeshall was a tall, well-spoken man perhaps sixty years old. I asked him first the name of the diarist, afraid that my hope for a new view of the Second Seminole War period would be ended by the name Cohen, Potter, Duncan, Bemrose, or other known writers of the period.

"Lt. Henry Prince," Mr. Coggeshall replied.

Prince? Who in the world was Henry Prince? Certainly no one that I had come across in several years of research.

Had I understood correctly that what he had was an original diary, not a photocopy, photostat, typescript?

Yes, the diary was in longhand, several hundred pages, mostly in ink, some in pencil. Small handwriting, but generally quite legible. Small pages, perhaps four or five inches square, loose. A great many maps of the military roads, sketches of Ft. Brooke, Ft. Foster, that sort of thing. I asked how he had come by this diary.

"It was found in a trunk in the attic of the home of Dr. C. A. Van Slyke, by his daughter, my wife [Lucile M. Van Slyke], following his death in 1940.

"The Van Slyke family were pioneers from Cooperstown, New York, who settled in St. Paul, Minnesota, in 1854. Our guess is that

Prince was a friend of someone in the Van Slyke family and left the diary with them for safekeeping while he was away with the Army during the Civil War. He probably just neglected to come back for it."

Carefully I asked if Mr. Coggeshall and his wife would consider selling the diary in order for it to be brought back to Florida and made available to researchers.

Well, they would think about it. They were in Florida on vacation from their home in New Jersey and would be returning there within a few weeks. They would let me know.

During November and December I talked to Mr. Coggeshall a number of times on the phone and we exchanged several letters. He sent me a sample of a dozen or so photocopied pages. I was distressed to see that someone, perhaps in an effort to clarify occasional dates and names, had made bold emendations with a ballpoint pen here and there across the faint original writing. It was unfortunate, but not a serious threat to the integrity of the work. A typical page contained 36 lines of handwriting, averaging eight words to the line, a total of 288 words per page. If there were even 100 pages of text it would mean nearly 30,000 words of a West Point, eyewitness account of the Seminole War. Words unknown to the field of Florida history.

On the 17th of December 1978, Mr. Coggeshall wrote that he and his wife had decided to offer the diary for sale. On the 9th of January my wife Dale Anne, our two small daughters, Amie and Jodi, and I arrived at the Coggeshall home. Mr. Coggeshall brought out a packet of paper perhaps an inch and a half thick and set it before me. The Diary. Winter sunlight seemed to glow on the little pile of paper. I touched it, turned back a paper cover. I read "1836 – Land of Flowers. Aim to 'gather laurels'. January 10." Tomorrow it would be exactly 142 years since Henry Prince, 2nd Lieutenant, 4th Infantry Regiment, U.S. Army, had written these opening words at St. Augustine, Florida. I turned more pages, caught glimpses of places, men, battles. Here was no dry, indifferent account of nameless places, faceless men, battles reckoned only by whether they were won or lost. Here was life, color, detail. It was apparent that Henry Prince had been a participant in, as well as an interested observer of, the events through which the land of the Seminoles had been taken from them, blacks returned to slavery, thousands of lives lost, Florida set on the road that would transform it from a battleground into a nation's playground.

Henry Prince had met many of the leading participants during the tragic drama of the Second Seminole War: Osceola, Micanopy, Zachary Taylor, Clinch, Gaines, Dade. Prince had designed Ft. Foster, described by his commanding officer as "one of the strongest and best field fortifications ever erected (against Indians) on this continent." A drawing of the Fort filled a page. Prince had mapped the course of the Withlacoochee River from Ft. Dade to Ft. Cooper. From the window of the tower where I write, I would have seen him pass. He wrote of swimming in these same dark and lovely waters that still hurry past my home. He had quartered at Ft. Dade, traveled up and down the Ft. King Road, visited and sketched the graves of Dade's command when the graves were new. He had visited Powel's (Osceola's) Town, the now legendary refuge of the Indian leader in the "Cove of the Withlacoochee," and described it in minute detail. He had traveled Florida from the Atlantic to the Gulf, from Georgia to Key West. And all that he experienced he described—sometimes briefly as circumstances of battle or march allowed, sometimes with vivid simile: "the bullets twitter over our heads like a rush of blackbirds" (during Gaines's battle at the Withlacoochee, 5 March 1836). This young officer who "aimed to gather laurels" had gathered wounds instead.

Mr. Coggeshall was as concerned as I that the diary return to Florida, be available for research. He named a modest price. I wrote a check.

Back home, Dale and I faced the task of preparing the diary for publication. Clearly the first step was to photocopy the entire work to reduce the wear and tear on the original. Jay Dobkin of the Special Collections Department of the University of South Florida in Tampa kindly accepted this chore. Then, with the original safely bagged, copy in hand, I began reading the diary aloud while Dale made a new handscript, line for line, page for page as Prince had written it. (In 1979 computers were distant, at least on our horizon.) Though Prince generally had written with a clear and legible hand, the stress of events, the weather, time, had all caused words to blur, an occasional lapse of capital letters and punctuation, the loss of pages, problems with chronology. After a hundred evenings of this effort and only two diary months completed, we realized the need for assistance. Dr. John Mahon, Bill Goza, Don and Marsha Sheppard, Henry and Miriam Cohen, and others came to the rescue. Over a period of years our joint efforts produced first a complete handscript, then a typescript, with once again a complete reading against the photocopy to insure the highest accuracy possible.

William M. Goza, past president of the Florida Historical and Florida Anthropological Societies, recipient of an award from the American Association for State and Local History for his contributions to the preservation and interpretation of Florida history, teacher, author, attorney, and close friend, had, from the first mention of the Prince diary, realized its value and importance. With the first typescript completed, Goza made arrangements for a refund of our payment to Mr. Coggeshall and the permanent placement of the original diary and a copy of the typescript with Elizabeth Alexander, curator of the Department of Special Collections, P. K. Yonge Library of Florida History, at the University of Florida in Gainesville. Since the retirement of Ms. Alexander, her invaluable cooperation has been continued by her successor, James Cusick.

It was 1990 before the acquisition of a computer allowed us to begin the transfer of the typescript to a disk. That task well done by Donna Clark, the editing of the diary could finally get underway. The guiding principle has been to leave the work essentially as Henry Prince wrote it. Thus the editing has been a matter of standardizing the dating, eliminating words that Prince had crossed out, applying a few capital letters and the occasional comma or period, these additions indicated by brackets. We have, for the most part, left Prince's idiosyncratic spelling ("waggon" or "wagon;" "Miconapi" or "Miccanopy," etc.) as he spelled them, without change or repetitious use of "sic." Bill Dayton, friend and local attorney, was of great help in translating foreign words and phrases used by Prince. And from first computer encounter to final printing, Kitty Szaro of Trilby has guided, corrected, and rescued us from fatal errors. Our debt to her is great.

As the handscripts and typescripts struggled toward completion, a steady dispatch of queries had been sent across the country seeking background information on this Henry Prince. Who was he, where had he come from, where did he go? The Coggeshalls had told us that the William Van Slyke (with whom Prince had left his diary) Papers were held by the Minnesota Historical Society. From the large collection of Prince material contained within the Van Slyke Papers kindly supplied by Dallas Lindgren, Head of Reference Services, Division of Archives and Manuscripts at the Society, we learned much of Prince, including his birthplace, Eastport, Maine.

Margot McCain and M. K. Murphy, librarians for the Maine Historical Society, and Hugh French, chairman of the Waterfront Research Committee in Eastport, provided us with a wealth of information about Eastport itself, the area that Prince had known as a child and young man. Still living in Eastport he had received an appointment to the military academy in 1831. The United States Military Academy (West Point) Library provided records of his cadet years as well as his military career beyond the Florida War.

The Prince letters from the Van Slyke collection lightly covered the years 1847 through 1859. Lee Johnson, assistant director of the Center for Polar and Scientific Archives, National Archives and Records Service, Washington, D.C., found a file of official letters and reports authored by Prince in 1854. The Military Service Records as well as the Center for Cartographic and Architectural Archives departments of the General Services Administration supplied additional maps of Florida sites drawn by Prince, as well as correspondence, military and personal, from the years 1860 through 1889. Finally, for 1892, we were able to accumulate a file relating to his death in London. Copies of the obituaries from five London papers gave us the details.

From the material gathered across these twenty years we have drawn a sketch of the life of Henry Prince prior to 1836, an introduction to the Diary. The epilogue takes up his life from the Diary's end to his death fifty years later.

Some forty drawings done in the field by Prince, some in pencil, some in ink, illustrate many of the places he visited, the routes he traveled. The pencil drawings especially have faded. The task of bringing these out of the shadows in remarkably clear photographs has been done by Greg Cunningham of the Office of Instructional Resources, University of Florida, Gainesville. As a result, it has been possible to reproduce every drawing and, as near as possible, present it in its proper order within the text. And rather than attempt to remove the recent ballpoint datings from the original pages, Michael Christopher, also of Gainesville, has magically removed them from the photographs through computer manipulation.

The publication of this extraordinary diary, long awaited by the many contributors of labor, skill, and encouragement through the years of preparation, as well as historians, reenactors, and those who have simply heard of the work in progress, has been handsomely done by the University of Tampa Press. Our editors, Richard Mathews and Ellen White, have helped at all times and hours in those ways in which only an editor *can* help.

The Seminole Wars Historic Foundation Inc. is operated exclusively for charitable, educational, and civic purposes related to its subject. Since the start of the Foundation in mid-1992, board president Judith McCurdy Altenhoff, members Norman Altenhoff, James W. Covington, Ph.D., Billy Cypress, Dale Anne Laumer, John K. Mahon, Ph.D., J. Crayton Pruitt, M.D., and Brent Weisman. Ph.D., have encouraged publication of Prince's Diary. Doctors Covington, Mahon, and Weisman have each studied the entire work and from their vast knowledge of the subject matter have aided the editing greatly through explanations of arcane references and particularly through recommendations for specific inclusions and exclusions of notes. Finally, in the critical matter of cost, the Foundation has supplied the funds which have made a reality of the entire effort.

–Frank Laumer
Talisman
Dade City, Florida
July 1998

INTRODUCTION

Brevet 2nd Lieutenant Henry Prince, 4th Infantry Regiment, U.S. Army, first came to the Florida Territory in January 1836. He was 25 years old, six months out of West Point, a thousand miles from home. He called this wilderness the "Land of Flowers" and confided to his diary that he aimed "to gather laurels."

On January 10th he left St. Augustine, arrived at Fort Drane on the 15th, and was assigned to Company D. Around him lay wounded soldiers brought back from General Clinch's encounter two weeks before with Seminole Indians at the Withlacoochee River (a "battle" or "skirmish" depending on whether you were there or not). On the 15th he "heard that Maj. Dade's command was cut off attempting to march from Tampa to Fort King." On Sunday the 31st, across the camp "[Lt.] Ward is shot in the belly with buck shot at about 15 paces by Col[.] Parish. He received the whole charge—screamed O Lord and fell perfectly torn open."

That evening Prince wrote in his diary: "It is strange how soon familiarity . . . will soften the dread and remove . . . the terror of Death. I have had little [familiarity] of it compared to many but that, however little, has come all at once. Here I am in an enemy's country where life is worth nothing, not more than a dry leaf—and every comer like a gust of Autumnal wind brings the certain intelligence that some [more men] have fallen in an indifferent, reckless and contemptuous rush. The entire company (that I came here to join . . .), every individual life, has been taken! . . . But death belongs to the human family! . . . What is it to die . . . to be shot in some vital part and suffer no more!"

Fifty-six long years later, retired Colonel (and Brigadier General by brevet) Henry Prince was alone in his room in Morley's Hotel, Trafalgar Square, London. Lucy Player, chambermaid, had just brought the old man a cup of beef tea. It was nine o'clock. Prince sat in a chair by his bed writing.

"When an individual life has run its cycle and become a waste of nature in the body, overwhelming its mental and physical qualities with weakness and pain to an intolerable degree, It may with all propriety be removed . . ." Eighty-one years old, in constant pain from wounds received so long ago in the Florida War, in the war with Mexico, and again in the battle of Cedar Mountain, Virginia, during the Civil War, suffering from Bright's disease, he had tried for months to convince himself to go back home. He dreaded the sea voyage; he had no family to return to. He finished his letter, put it in an unsealed envelope, addressed it "To All Friends," and laid it on top of two others. He picked up a revolver purchased two days before. He lay back in his chair, put the gun to his right temple, squeezed the trigger.

Henry Prince was born on January 19, 1811, the son of Benjamin and Sarah (Webster) Prince. His birthplace was the village of Eastport on Moose Island, Massachusetts (later to become Eastport, Maine). The island was four-and-a-half miles long and just over a mile wide, lying a thousand feet off the mainland in Passamaquoddy Bay. "The village is pleasantly situated on the southerly and easterly part of the island, facing the harbor . . . It presents a fine view, particularly in approaching it from the eastward: there is a regular ascent from the water to the rear of the village. From the garrison, on Fort Hill, are presented some delightful views and landscapes for the pencil of the painter, as well as the admirers of nature."

The garrison, Fort Sullivan, had been built in 1808, partly to restrain British naval activity in the Bay but more to control smuggling, the most popular enterprise of the international community around the Bay. It was successful at neither. In July 1814 a British fleet appeared in the Bay, demanded the fort's surrender, and was accommodated within five minutes. One thousand troops were landed among a population only slightly larger. The occupation, which lasted throughout the war, was for the most part peaceful, the English no more able to control the smuggling than the American authorities had been. Henry Prince recalled many years later his delight and pride on the morning of June 30, 1818, when at seven years old he stood with the others at the fort to watch the English flag come down for the last time, to be replaced by the Stars and

Stripes. All question of sovereignty of the island had been settled by a commission six months before, and Eastport was now the easternmost community of the easternmost point of the United States.

Moose Island had first been visited by Europeans in the early 1600s, but only after the American Revolution did permanent settlement become a reality. In 1783 the five families on the island made a living taking and curing fish. By the time of Prince's birth, the population had grown to more that 1,500. Progress was slow. A horse had been brought over on the ferry in 1804. It "excited curiosity and even fear" in the inhabitants. Back in 1799 a road had been laid out in a charmingly casual way, "Beginning at Mr. James Cochran's spring . . . and running northerly between said Cochran's house and his old hovel, and just to the westward of Mr. Samuel Tuttle's barn, through the corner of his potatoe field." Without horses, and hence without a wagon or a carriage, there was not much use to a road, and by 1835 "it would be impossible to say where it was." Most travel was by boat, and settlers had built wherever it suited their convenience with little thought to future development. Paths "irregular and contracted" served the purpose of leading from cabin to cabin and down to the sea.

With the end of war and withdrawal of the English to their own lands across the Bay, life quickened all around the Bay and up and down the St. Croix River which fed it. Less than a month after the change of flags the Eastport *Sentinel* was established, and in 1819 the St. Andrews *Herald*. Virgin timber was being cut in prodigious amounts on both sides of the river; "forty–seven small mills with single or double saws [were] in full operation cutting 7,000,000 feet of timber annually." In 1820 a bridge 1,200 feet long was built connecting Moose Island with the mainland. Mail was coming over once a week and soon twice, three times, and by 1833, daily. The Bank of Passamaquoddy was established in Eastport in 1820 with capital of $100,000. Since 1785 there had been talk all over the northeastern part of the state of separation from Massachusetts. The move was voted down year after year, but by an ever smaller margin. Finally, in October 1819 a convention was called, a constitution formed, and a general vote taken. On 15 March 1820 Maine came into the Union as the twenty–third state.

These years of Prince's childhood, like the next decade of his boy-hood, were lived in both splendid isolation and boisterous confusion of growth, for both the boy and the community. The military pres-ence, both English and American, was a constant and active part of the legal, economic, and social life of the island and its town. As Eastport was growing, so was its excellent harbor. Shipbuilding along with shipping itself (legal and otherwise) took on a vigorous life. Until 1821 only three foreign vessels had entered the port (excepting the English), but ten years later more than 800 ships of foreign registry dropped anchor in a single year. Fort Sullivan stood guard on its hill-top, the American flag snapping in the breeze. Under English occupa-tion a touch of glamour had been added to the isolated frontier village; balls had been given, a theatre organized, horse races held. Soldiers were a part of Eastport. Now American soldiers drawn from many states occupied the Fort and became a presence in the town. Uni-form, drill, color, and order were in stark contrast to the rough, care-less ways of civilian life in a boomtown of the early nineteenth century.

After the first years of settlement, barren of every effort but the struggle to survive, attempts had been made here and there about the tiny community to provide some kind of schooling. There were few trained teachers available, no building for a school, little money to pay the costs. In those early days one experiment had been a two–room building, half tavern and half classroom. "Mr. Greenwood was proprietor of both, and performed the duties of barkeeper in one and teacher . . . in the other . . . And although he may have . . . intended to spend the larger portion of his time in the school room during the hours appropriated for teaching, yet he would occasion-ally hear the call of some patrons of the other room, "Here, old man, fill this pitcher!" And, as that side of the house was the most difficult to please, he would very promptly obey the summons; . . . the scholars . . . during his absense [sic] . . . would recreate [sic] themselves with an eight–handed reel, and, as the music was by gen-eral chorus, it would often serve for both rooms."

"For some years after this experiment [1793–94] Eastport showed little interest in schools. Some were unkind enough to suggest that one could attain a high degree of competence as a fisherman or a smuggler without the formal education."

Since those early years, the struggle to provide food, clothing, and shelter in spite of deprivation and bitter weather had more than succeeded. By 1820 "Eastport settled down to enjoy prosperity such as she has never known since." Or had ever known before. That year "over $60,000 was spent in wharves, warehouses, and stores." Not bad for a community of less than 2,000. Nor had they forgotten education. With (comparative) prosperity had come schools, both public and private. The "public" schools provided elementary education. In the private schools "instruction is given in the higher branches of education, to youth of both sexes, separate from each other." Though his family was of modest circumstances, Henry Prince attended the Gardiner Lyceum, "one of our most distinguished literary Institutions," for two years, probably 1829 and 1830. "He there exhibited good talents and a commendable proficiency in Chemistry, Elements of Natural History and in Mathematics. His deportment was gentlemanly and his moral character unimpeachable." During this time he gained practical knowledge of business by working as accountant and secretary for several Eastport business houses, a boy who looked to a future beyond fishing, woodcutting, or smuggling.

There was little chance that Prince could go on to college. "[His] pecuniary means are too limited to afford him the opportunity of obtaining an education at one of our Northern Semenaries [sic]." Unless of course he could get an appointment to West Point. There existed vacancies to be filled by the new state of Maine, "she not having her relative proportion at that Institution." On January 12, 1831, one week before his nineteenth birthday, Prince wrote to the Secretary of War offering himself as a candidate for the appointment of cadet. Six anxious months later he received the hoped–for appointment, responding that "[I] shall repair to Westpoint [sic] immediately and report myself to the Superintendent of the Military Academy."[1]

The superintendent was Major Sylvanus Thayer, himself the thirty–third graduate of the Academy, class of 1808, and termed "Father of the Military Academy." Prince passed the oral examination then required and was admitted as a cadet on September 1, 1831. As the four years of rigorous training whittled down their ranks from ninety-seven to fifty-six through resignation or dismissal, Prince, who had finished his first year in the lower fourth of his class, gained a little ground each year to graduate thirtieth in order of merit. On July 1st, 1835, he was promoted in the army to Brevet Second Lieutenant, assigned to the 4th Infantry Regiment. By the end of the year he was in Florida.

For a young man from Maine the weather must have been the first surprise. No wonder that after twenty years of Arctic winters he thought this the "Land of Flowers." The temperature was in the mid-70s and the world was green. (He had probably not yet heard that the previous February the cold had been so severe that it was said that every citrus tree north of Tampa Bay had frozen.)

Florida had been a Territory for only fifteen years, the population of its thirty-seven million acres amounting to less than 50,000 (including slaves and Seminole Indians), not quite one person for every square mile of wilderness. Still, that was crowded enough for war. During the December just past, hostilities had broken out here and there, culminating in the annihilation of two companies of American soldiers (including five West Point officers) under Brevet Major Francis Dade barely two weeks ago. The hue and cry had been raised, regulars and volunteers were coming to the rescue of wild–eyed settlers who had preempted Seminole land, to help the "slave–chasers" return blacks to bondage.

Lt. Henry Prince was in St. Augustine, close to the northeast corner of a territory that extended 350 miles west, 400 south. He was about to leave the first permanent European settlement in the United States and march into a wilderness. He hoped to "gather laurels." On January 10, he began a diary.

THE DIARY OF LT. HENRY PRINCE

I'll take no more such rides - A man's
left too much to his own reflections & they
too often fail to be amusing - Tampa looks
very pretty when first you come in sight of
it getting out of the woods - The river the
buildings the bay Gadsdens point, beyond it -
all striking - a very level & simple view but
vast & brilliant - so much water & so many
white houses - Very canoe full of drunk"

(19th) Out in the bushes doing this -

while the working party is gathering and burning twigs!
Some attempts made by 2 miscreants to set up
an establishment in the bay for trading grog
to soldiers & powder & lead to the Indians.
Tampa - Flirt followed me - She got very
tired & when I would ride up to a big log she
would get onto the log & jump into the saddle
then she would ride along with me & go
to sleep. It is not pleasant riding alone
in such a dreary & monotonous country,

I'll take no more such rides - A man's
left too much to his own reflections & they
too often fail to be amusing - Tampa looks
very pretty when first you come in sight of
it getting out of the woods - The river the

1836 ——— Land of Flowers — to "gather
Laurels" — January 10 — at 1/4 12 left
St Augustine — 4½ at Picolata — were one
hour crossing the St Johns 2½ miles wide.
The fires looked splendid as we entered the
bivouac.

11th. Waited for Lt Dancy — Saw a burning 5 m

12th. Waked at 5 oc to be informed that a dog
had been heard to bark not far off. We were
on the qui vive. Directly a pack of wolves shot
past a picket fire with a noise compared to which
the Eastport Band's was music! Started on march
towards Micanopi. Halted at 12 there being
4 waggons in rear. 1/45 they came up.

13th. 20' to 8 in full march — 3 waggons broke
down — a new axletree was made for one — in
spite of which at 7¾ we had gained 17 miles. We
prepared for an attack passing through the Scrub

14th False alarm in the evening — sentinel fired
— I saw a hog — lost Pot Withers pencil.

15th. Marched 25 miles encumbered with 15
waggons — Arrived at the Lang Syne picketifi=
=cation — assigned to duty with [D] comp[y] 4th Inf
The capt wounded — Lieu Graham commanding.

21st Heard that Maj Dade's command was cut
off attempting to march from Tampa to Ft King

22 nd. Waggoner Convoy gone to Picolata —

23 d. Off Day — False alarm at midnight occasioned

1. Opening page of the Diary of Lt. Henry Prince

THE DIARY OF LT. HENRY PRINCE

1836

Land of Flowers[. A]im to "gather laurels[.]"

January

10th. At 1/4 12 left St. Augustine — 4 1/2 at Picolata[1] — were one hour crossing the St. Johns 2 1/2 miles wide. The fires looked splendid as we entered the bivouac.

11th. Waited for Lt. Dancy[2] — Saw a burning 5 m[iles].

12th. Waked at 5 o'c to be informed that a dog had been heard to bark not far off. We were on the qui vive.[3] Directly a pack of wolves shot past a picket fire with a noise compared to which the Eastport Band's was music! Started on march towards Micanopi.[4] Halted at 12 there being 4 waggons in rear. 1/4 5 they came up.

13th. 20' to 8 in full march — 3 waggons broke down — a new axletree was made for one — in spite of which at 7 1/4 we had gained 17 miles. We prepared for an attack passing through the scrub.

14th. False alarm in the evening — Sentinel fired — I saw a hog — lost Pvt. Withers' pencil.

15th. Marched 25 miles encumbered with 15 waggons — Arrived at the Lang Syne picketification[5] — Assigned to duty with (D) compy. 4th Inf. The capt. wounded — Jno Graham[6] commanding.

21st. Heard that Maj. Dade's command was cut off[7] attempting to march from Tampa[8] to Ft. King.[9]

22nd. Convoy gone to Picolata.

23rd. Off[icer of the] Day. False alarm at midnight occasioned by a

sentinel at the sugar house firing on the patrol without challenging —
he shot the Sergeant & broke his leg above the ankle joint. During the
day the volunteers <u>fired by company</u> & occasioned some bustle.

24th. 4 companies under Col. Twiggs[10] have sailed from N. Orleans. Capt. Porter's at St. Augustine.

25th. Nothing special except that the volunteers shot a hog in the
night.

26th. Commenced drill.

30th. Express arrived from Ft. King — no news — Ward[11] is arrested. Mail came yesterday — and such a mail! — old threadbare
papers. They contain some slight suspicion that the Indians will get
mad and be immediately restored to good nature. Congress too has
most munificently voted 80,000 dollars — to kill them all with if they
should happen to be obstinate. It wouldn't buy provisions enough to
stay the stomacks of the musquitoes that harrass the army now — little
as it is.

31st. Sunday. Offr. Day. Ward is shot in the belly with buck shot at
about 15 paces by Col. Parish.[12] He received the whole charge —
screamed O Lord and fell perfectly torn open. The account that I have
of it is; Yesterday Parish wished to put him on duty that is performed
by tours when it was not his tour. Ward refused to do it. P. arrested
him. He wouldn't obey the arrest and today the guards were ordered
to take him in custody. He took 3 pistols from his tent saying that he
would shoot the first man that laid hands on him. At this Parish said
something and Ward flirting his fist said "You — God damn you." He
did not shake his fist towards P. he merely made a gesture with it, rais-
ing it & bringing it down forcibly. Then it was that Parish discharged
a musket into him. He was perhaps 15 minutes dying. I heard the gun
but of course was not aware of the dread messenger it hurled to the
only acquaintance I had in the "mounted volunteers." (10 o'clock)

General Call[13] with 500 foot is on his march here — Ward, it is said,
has a brother coming with him. Col. Parish has left his camp and stays
inside of the pickets. Inquest in session all the after noon. The high
(volunteer) officers appear to be all of the opinion that Parish did right.
The privates do not.

Evening. Just heard Parish relate the affair. "I was in fact attached
to his family in Tallahassee — been acquainted with his brother there

this 10 years. I went to him yesterday and talked to him in a friendly way — had quite a long talk with him — I pretended not to be aware of his obstinacy. He had said that he would not stay in his tent. I told the Sergeant of the guard to make him go to his tent & disarm him. He took a file of men and Ward said he would go to his tent — but in order to make better preparations. He went in & Capt Holstein came to me & says he, "he will shoot you" & said I, "what can I do; here I am without any gun." He offered me his gun — said it was loaded. There was a double barrelled gun laying in the tent then. I slipped the cover off of it and ran out thinking I could get into his tent before he left & tie him. He had gone round his tent & got nearly between it and mine. I ordered him to go in — I told the men to take hold of him & disarm him — they said they were afraid to, they believed he would shoot them. "Well", says I,"God damn him, shoot <u>him</u>." He aimed his pistol at me. Says he, "God damn you I'll shoot <u>you</u>." And I — (He muttered this part. I thought he said — <u>drew up & stopped him.</u>)

It is strange how soon familiarity with him will soften the dread & remove or weaken the terror of Death. I have had little of it compared to many, but that, however little, has come all at once. Here I am in an enemies country where life is worth nothing — not more than a dry leaf — & every comer like a gust of Autumnal wind brings the certain intelligence that some have fallen in an indifferent, reckless & contemptuous rush. The entire company! (that I came here to join & regard as my <u>own</u> — or that to which <u>I belong</u>), every individual life, has been taken! Major Dade its Capt. who seems to me like one of <u>my own military family</u> is gone with it. Basinger & Mudge[14] whom I was well acquainted with — Henderson[15] & Ward with whom I have been intimate — are dead. But these are merely the ones that were nearest to me — that fell within the <u>most conspicuous</u> compass of my perceptions. I ought to say that I have not been <u>long</u> familiar with Death insted of saying <u>little</u>. But Death belongs to the human family! Like any of them that become famous he falls amazingly on a single unreserved acquaintance with him. What is it to die to be shot in some vital part and suffer no more!

I feel disagreable when I think of going into battle, not on account of what I may risk but the risk I cause to others. For my own part <u>I wish to go</u>, for others I feel sorry to. I hate to risk what's entirely devoted to others — entirely depended upon by them — entirely worth-less to myself. Entirely — <u>perhaps</u> I am wrong in saying entirely. It is certain that of all my rights I value my life the least (I would rather yield them all nevertheless than to suffer certain torments). But there would be difficulty in believing that from another. Every one will agree however that the man who <u>backs out</u> of his profession because he risks his life in it is apt to <u>back out</u> of his clothes and sure never to get any-thing for his employers — he can in fact go into no profession.

February

1st. Ward is buried today — Whiting[16] and myself joined onto the tail end of the procession.

4th. Went on command for Picolata with 16 baggage waggons. The guard consisted of 10 privates & 2 non com[missione]d officers. 13 of the teamsters were armed. Encamped at Daniels's.

5th. Went through the "Scrub" this day — encamped at the 21 mile post. False alarm in the night — occasioned by a bear approach-ing one of the Sentinels.

6th. Arrived at Picolata at 3 o'clock. The place — the river —the woods — are alive with troops & preparations for real war.

14th. After nearly 5 days fatigue marching arrived at Lang Syne again. Thankful that I am back alive! I learn that only a part of Maj. Dade's compy. is lost. The greater portion of it having been left at Tampa Bay. There were but 2 comps. then that lost themselves in en-deavoring to obey their orders. Maj. D's compy. had not been ordered to go to Camp King.

17th. When at Picolata Genl. Scott[17] was expected there daily. An express arrived last night from Tallahassy with news that 107 were killed in the battle of Ouithlacoutchy [Withlacoochee][18] — that Powel[19] received two shots & is recovering: that Genl. Gaines[20] is at Tampa with 1500 men & expecting Call to join him with 300 more. Scott is therefore on one side of the indians — Gaines on the other. When they meet there will be two Richmonds in the field.

> "Peace to the memory of the brave
> However they fall!
> Fame shall the warriors aches lave
> His deeds recall."

Yesterday Capt. Dranes[21] company moved over to Mackintosh's.

18th. Marched to Ft. King (the King of Forts in these parts) 4 compys. & a field p[iece]. — got brilliantly wet! Breakfasted at reveille, dived at Flotards,[22] dried supped & luxuriated at fort K. No fresh tracks of Indians were observed on the way. The road does not thread many hammocks or scrubbs. To my surprise we did not receive three cheers on heaving in sight — Nevertheless, our reception was warm & comfortable.

19th. Two companies cleared a trail which avoids the hammock west of the Ft. The fort is a pleasant place but the officers are discontented on account of its dangers.

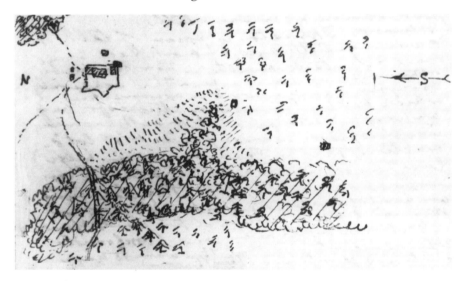

2. Fort King

Gen. Thompson[23] & Smith[24] were killed between Rog[er]s[25] house & the fort. Rogers 400 yards beyond his house, he ran in the wrong direction otherwise he would have saved himself as did others. About 60 chosen tall Indians laid in the scrub for 2 days. Cudgo[26] says the Indians "drew T.s spirit". He was not in the habit of going to R's house about the time but heedlessly took a stroll that way on the day. T & S. were not robbed but they had leisure to rob Rogs.

20th. Returned to Lang Syne — learn that a party of Indians were yesterday at Micanopy, they killed one man & wounded one. This confirms the report that the waggons were beset on the last trip.

21st. Off. Day. Lts. Graham, Dancy & Lee[27] very bad scared at one of the guns of their own party.

22nd. Celebration in the woods — the bosom of nature moved with pleasure. The [B]lues[28] give a talk & a procession — also eat their pork & bread off the same table. Thruston[29] is a man of talk & cunning — Little eyes — Shrunk face, small nose & contack mouth! How can he be otherwise. Lee is a man that occasionly brings in a large word in conversation which has been previously studied for half an hour — & then he does it with such an in— appropriate accompaniment (of look & action) that no "knowing one" can help laughing at his indiscretion! To my surprise the officers of the Regulars received an invitation to take port with them for they had dippers enough if two would drink out of one. Still more was I confounded when I ascertained that they were to have toasts! But my motto in this respect is that if I back out to [at least] back out "in the regular way". So I gave a toast & made at least a noisy retreat. The toast was: "The oration in the wilderness on the birthday of Washington — a glorious exaltation out of the very bosom of nature." There were many good toasts and much good feeling displayed. Wine was the only beverage drunk. Gen. Clynch[30] was not present but sent a toast complimenting the Blues. An ensign was hoisted made of silk handkerchiefs by some members of the Blues. The flag staff was surmounted by a scotch liberty cap. The table was broken up by retreat drum calling all hands to parade. The orator was Lt. Harris of the Richmond Blues who at home is a Lawyer & attorney genl. of the State of Georgia. A company of mounted men (27 in number) under Capt. Lancaster stopped to rest the night here. They are on their way to St. Augustine & bring no intelligence except that Genl. Call's troops were at St. Marks[31] ready to embark a week ago for Tampa. Gen. Call told Capt. Lancaster that it was doubtful whether he should take the field at all — that he did not like to do so with diminished rank beneath what the [President] had conferred on him — & that if he did enter the field it would be as a private. They say that 3 or 400 warriors are missing out of the Creek Nation — It is presumed they have joined the Sem[inole]s.

The report (see 31st Jan) respecting Gen. Call was false though believed at the time — ditto (24th) respecting Lt. Col. Twiggs.

23rd. I have omitted to record the toast of Private ____ of the Blues:

> Our Star Spangled Banner — Though it be homely
> Does just as well as if it were comely
> And proves that our boys ever on the alert
> Can soon make a shift if they can't make a shirt.

Afternoon. Lolling on the bed. Jno. Graham, reading funny stories out of the N. York Mirror — everything else in print having been exhausted. We were soon tired out on that litterary road. Well, we talked. "I would, says G., give 200$ out of my own pocket if Gaines was here — (soldiers running & bellowing & congratulating outside) — What's that? continued G., — (we both listened & heard): "O how thick they are!" "Genl. Gaines is coming!" "Hurra!" — Says I "I'll take the 200$."

This arrival was Col. Foster[32] with 7 companies of the 4th Infy. — 250 men from Fort King where they left Genl G. with the rest of the force (1000 more) with which he has just completed his march from Tampa. The troops hove in sight about 4 o'clock.

Amongst the officers I recognised Henry Scott,[33] Mitchell,[34] Ben Alvord[35] & Abram Myers.[36] [They] Left Ft. King at sunrise arrived at Lang Syne at 3 1/2.

The whole command [Col. Foster under Gen. Gaines} left Tampa Bay on the 13th inst. with 1200 men — about 800 being volunteers from N. Orleans whose expenses were paid by an appropriation of 75,000$ be. Leg Louis [?] 5000 subscription citizens. Citizens of N. Orleans raised about 5000$ subscription for the widows of Dades Massacre. All the regulars have left N. Orleans & Baton Rouge. [Gaines command marched] 7 miles [on 13th]. On 14th they marched 10 miles to the river Alafia. The indians had burned all the houses on the road. 15th. Marched back this road towards Withla[coochee] & made 16 miles encamped at 4 1/2 o ck — 16th Marched 9 miles & forded the Hillsborough river — up to the hips. Reeve[37] was wounded in the thigh by his pistol exploding in his pocket, was hauled in cart. Volunteers became dissatisfied & threatened to go home[, d]isappointed the fighting was not what it was cracked up to be. 17th burnt an Indian Village — took the corn & hogs & rice. Supposed they heard a cannon. The Indians appear to have left their town in great precipitation for their provisions were bundled up [as] if to take away. 18th came to the big

Withlacoochee which they forded with amusement[,] pulling in the volunteers. One of the volunteers reported his Capt. to Gaines for drinking stronger coffee than the privates did. 19th discharged their muskets. Crossed the Little Withla[coochee][38] on a log. Burnt a small town near Dade's last encampment, the spot where they [Gaines command] encamped. 20th. Started abt. sunrise & at 8 1/2 o'clock came to the scene of massacre. A dreadful scene it was.

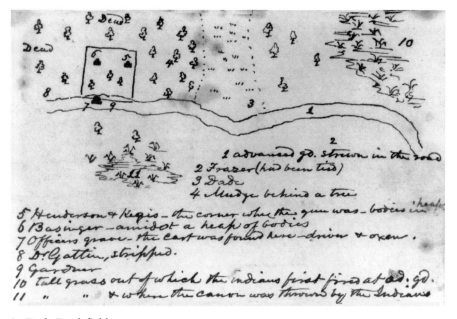

3. Dade Battlefield

    1. Advanced guard strewn in the road.
    2. Fraser[39] (had been tied).
    3. Dade
    4. Mudge behind a tree.
    5. Henderson & Keais[40] — the corner where the gun was — bodies in heap.
    6. Basinger — amidst a heap of bodies.
    7. Officer's grave — the cart was found here — driver & oxen.
    8. Dr. Gatlin,[41] stripped.
    9. Gardner [Gardiner][42]
    10. tall grass out of which the indians first fired at ad. gd.
    11. "   "   & where the cannon was thrown by the Indians

The rectangle was about 3 feet high of 3 tiers of logs[,] the side being the length of one log — it was on the highest part of the ground.

The scene can hardly be effaced from the memory of those who beheld it. The skeletons of the slain lay where they were shot. As the flesh was decayed it was difficult to decide whether they had been scalped. The ground was favorable to the troops being thickly timbered with pine trees without underbrush. The bodies of the officers were identified. Maj. Dade was found stripped between the adv. gd. & hd. of column. Capt. Fraser near him.

From the position of the body & of a rope near it, it is presumed he was tied. It was recognised by a breastpin in his bosom containing a beautiful miniature of himself painted by a brother officer. Lt. Mudge lay by a tree, two soldiers near him. It was recognised by the figure 3 on his cap — a ring on his finger & 5 gold pieces. Henderson and Keais were together. Left the Battle ground about noon. Marched 8 miles beyond Battle ground.

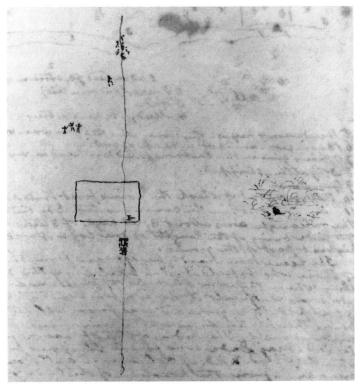

4. Dade Battlefield & the Fort King Road

21. Men sent in pursuit of cattle! Halted 13 miles from Ft. Kg.

22. Arrived at Ft. Kg.

24th. [Here Prince returns to his own chronology.] Relieved from duty at Ft. Drane[43] & took command of E company 4th Infantry for the day. I owe to D compy 4th Infy a sgts. sword old pattern without a scabbard. To Jno. Graham a dollar borrowed & for my messing from 16th Jany. to this date — excepting 10 days absent on command & also for a pair of sergeants pants.

At 2 o'clock Col. Foster's command started for Fort King arrived at 2 in the night. This was a forced march of the ugliest kind — but the weather was pleasant. The moon was in the zenith and sun just down as we left Flotards. The round shadows of the trees fell plum to the ground giving to the light & shadows a beautiful effect. There was a wide hollow of a mile in extent where the road was perfectly straight & terminated in a beautiful vista. To an observer in the rear the troops presented a sublime picture while they descended one branch & rose the other — the bright moonbeams glancing on their bayonets. The reflection too that we were in the Land of Flowers — and that the very stones in the road were adorned with the most splendid impresions of shells like the strap[?] table of a lady of taste to whom in some of her workmanship Dame nature bears a close resemblance.

We turned into the trail which leads a mile & a half from the road to Fort King through a pine barren avoiding a hammock, just after the moon sat. The trail was illuminated by glow—worms. The front guard here got separated from the pack horses & rear. After waiting some time it pushed on — pushed out of the trail amongst logs & brambles — the drunken Indians were called upon & finally led us up to Fort King. We marched into Gen. Gaines camp & bivouacked. The pack horses came up an hour afterwards & the rear guard — leaving the waggons in the rear which will be sent for in the morning. The men had they not had minds would have given out like the horses & oxen in the waggons.

26th. Received the property of Co B and took the command of it, 1st Lt. Page[44] being on leave, Lt. Alvord being in command of another company. 95 dollars & 5 cents compy. fund. There are 30 men here. 24 with arms. (2 with their arms will be left in the hospital [—] Gather & Hamilton. The Bugler & boy with Col. Foster. Mullen cook. Another victim of the hospital. 22 bearing arms in the ranks. This accounts for the whole thirty.)

The battallion was formed at 8 — at 9 or 10 we commenced the march for Withlacoochee. The main body advancing by center (as L[ight] I[nfantry] in one rank) preceeded by a 6 pdr. hauled by 4 horses. About a hundred men (mostly militia) on each side march as flankers. We marched 10 miles[,] a large part of the way through immense hammocks too thick with scrub to be dangerous. Abt. 1 1/2 miles from Rogers' house stood a neat shingled one story house with piazzas! Abt 8 miles passed through a deserted Indian & Negro town. Halted at 2 o'clock (10 miles) made a breast work three logs high. Junior Off gd (Alvord) for to night — 12 o'clock. Took my sleep the first half night. Wake by tremendous rain. Flemming did not stand with 2nd. Relief not to be found. I found him when the 3d went on & have got him standing under the sentinel on no 4.

27th. In full march at 7 o'clock. Passed a burial ground — saw horses over. Arrived at midday at a large town on the Withlacoochee. 16 houses — burnt it — track of 3 Indians seen — half an hour after I saw two bodies or rather skeletons on the right side of the road — one had soldiers brogans on — Gen'l Clinches killed, disenterred[. H]alted at the river to make preparations to cross — had halted 10 minutes when the action commenced on the left (we marched in 3 columns — volunteers on left — 4th Inf right, Arty &c centre). There was a constant crack for 3/4 of an hour [when] the firing ceased on both sides — we encamped[. O]ne killed & 6 wounded of volunteers — the killed was a frenchn. & served through Napoleons campaigns. The cannon fired 5 times. Several were scratched — a man at the cannon had the belly of his pants bored, the ball running tangent to his skin. While the drums were beating at gd. mounting (in the breastwork at evening, two hours after the battle) the Indians were heard discharging a "feu de joie"[45][. A]fter this all was silent for the night. All our fires were kept up all night. The yelling to day can hardly be called anything more than a yelp. I think I have heard a similar note made by blowing through the fingers. It was a shrill note (r—r—oo—oo—oo). When great numbers of them yelped it resembled a confused squealing.

28th. Sunday. Marched down the river about 3 miles to find a more advantageous place to cross. On approaching the river the Indians commenced a tremendous fire & squeal, both became louder & stronger as more entered into the contest. Halted to build block house for the wounded & a bridge & boats. The firing between the adv[ance] g[uar]d & Indians was kept up from 9 1/2 to 4. At the commencement of the action the guns went spitter spatter spitter spitter spitter spatter spatter spatter then whang! — whang! — then a big gun roaring & making the trees tremble. Short pauses & single guns till the time Capt. Armstrong[46] was wounded. Then a party on the left gave a distant shout or scream — as soon as they stopped the tribe near our front gave a tremendous reply, of more pretentions to effect than the little whi yi — the first syllable was shrill long & glided down the octave, the second was a short loud bass guteral sounded simultaneously by the whole tribe as if struck from one prodigious instrument. The word appeared to be Kirrr — wowh! Kirrr — wowh! Kirrr — wowh! wowgh! wowgh! wowgh! This ceremony was performed twice over — then both parties fired a rattling "feu de joie". After this all was silent for an hour — occasionally a rifle & a musket cracked almost in the same instant. Intermittent firing of single muskets & voleys of rifles till 4 when the indians appeared to have retired a little. The cannon was fired 7 times. They discharged their rifles about the same time that they did last night & in the same manner.

In the night there was much whooping — & some firing. I heard them receive one reinforcement. Suppose there were more. After the action was over we made a rectangular breastwork each company make

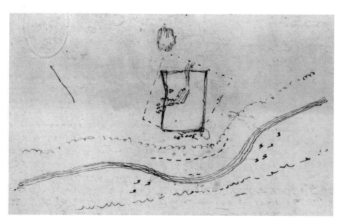

a portion — the length of its own line. The dotted lines are outside — the hatchets [represent] Indians, the double lines the fortifications 3 logs high. [Δ] [marks] my own tent.

5. Barricaded area that would be called Camp/Fort Izard

Monday 29th. Detailed to take charge of a fatigue party. They toted logs to the river to build a blockhouse. About 9 AM the cannon was fired, as the Gen. was going to reconnoitre, to scan the enemy from the opposite side of the river should he happen to be there. No sound of them was heard & had not been heard since night. I was out where the circle & dot is a hundred yds. from the works with a rifle and saw the tree hit behind which a sentinel was stationed.

6. Camp/Fort Izard

Lt. Linnard[47] came up a moment afterwards and we commenced a discussion whether there were any indians here or not. He supposed they had left. I told him of the shot of the sentinel. Whang! Whang! pop! fit! whirr! bang! spatter spatter spatter! It is no use to discuss it any longer says I for there they are. I ran to my line company amidst a storm of bullets. The Indians were round us as represented by the dots. There were at least 1000[. T]hey kept at a long distance. The fight was a very smart one for 3 hours. We did not fire away one tenth so much ammunition as they did what we did throw was not thrown away. I saw 8 or 10 indians. Had a full view of one fellow standing up at aim behind a large pine — drew a sight on him & fired — but the gun flashed in the pan.[48] The wind was in the direction of <u>the arrow</u>. At the tail of the arrow the indians set fire to the palmettos with which the ground was covered both outside of the breastwork & inside. It was extinguished as fast as it reached the breastwork by throwing over sand. It seems to me impossible for bullets to fly thicker anywhere then they did round me. They would cut holes through the palmetto leaves 3 feet from us while others would fall dead all round me. I was hit by two spent balls one in the hip & one in the back. Neither tore my clothes. I have both bullets in my pocket. My hip is quite sore.

This hot action displayed the faults of our breastwork and the use of it. When the firing ceased the breastwork was raised higher & defiled from reverse fire. The cannon fired 5 times during the action. One sergt. of regulars was killed — there were 19 men wounded. 6 or 8 horses killed & stolen. Two parties returned in the evening whooped & then fired a voley or two. While the music was beating at reveille a few rifles popped off on the other side of the river. The day & night beautiful warm & pleasant. Yesterday was pleasant. The day before wet — many cartridges were spoiled.

When outside with my rifle on my shoulder in the morning a volunteer passed by me & stopped. Says he to me "I spose it agin orders to pass out 'o here aint it sentinel?" — "I am not a sentinel." "O no! I mough 'o known that by your stripes sergeant," says he.

A spent ball knocked out Gen. Gaines' only tooth. Two men were wounded by the side of me one through the fleshy part of the cheek — the other through the right wrist. The latter I bound up with my towel which I carried in my pocket. A volunteer near me carried a cleaver, a rifle ball passed through the leather sheath. The thick leather waist belt of Sgt. Penn of my company was perforated by a ball which broke its force[. H]e was hurt but not injured. A White man was seen amongst the Indians.

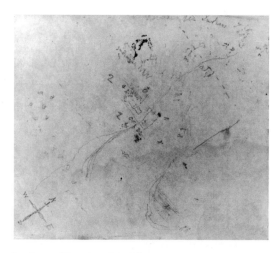

7. Camp/Fort Izard (with compass points)

March

1st. The body of an Indian killed by grape shot is reported to be in the hammock where he was dragged by the Indians. Ah! here comes a soldier with some accoutrements. I'll go & see them...powder horn of the very best rifle powder, leather haversack containing large quantity of bullets, pick brush & chain belonging to a musket, flints and other little things. The Indian was brought into camp. Did not go to see him. He was scalped by the volunteer that was wounded in the cheek yesterday. A cloud of turkey buzzards is hanging over a particular spot on the other side of the river.

At midday we saw Indians through the trees 400 yds. distant. They were in the direction N. of the fort and going West in single file. I suppose there were three hundred. I counted 30 & think the whole was more than 10 times as long passing as the 30 were. A thousand conjectures are afloat. The recall has been sounded all hands are inside & on the lookout.

Up all night, the Indians made a great deal of noise. I heard one making a speech at the full stretch of his voice. I heard every word plainly and distincly — one sentence terminated in "momis tah". At the end of his speech several muskets and rifles were discharged & a ball whirled by my ear into the fort. The sentinels were so much alarmed at the behaviour of the Indians that they ran in twice — some fired. At 2 o'clock it commenced raining and everything hushed up but the wind & water —even the tremendous fires in the woods went down.

Reveille waked up & popped off 2 rifles on these.[?]

2nd. Working parties on the N West side of the fort were fired on by a party in the hammock on this side. I slept nearly all day. It is remarkable that no guns were heard from the Indians at reveille — our fires were put out at night.

3rd. At 9 or 10 the General intending to reconnoitre caused the cannon to be dragged to the river & fired twice — he said it would serve one good purpose viz., tell our friends where we are if we have any at hand. One compy. of volunteers & [one of] 4th Inf. were extended in the hammock in front. About 1/2 an hour after the cannon had fired the Indians rushed upon the working party out on the Infy. front & drove them in — but hit <u>none</u> of them. The compys. in the hammock came in. The right compy (A) nearly reached to where the Indians left was. The Indians being dressed like regular soldiers, some having blue great coats, some even the forage cap — many having short blue jackets and trowsers,[49] approached the 4th. Infy. front very boldly and endeavored to make us think they were fighting there with some of our men[. T]hey would run in towards the fort (Fort Izard[50] by the by), take the near side of the tree and fire <u>back</u>! We were completely deceived for some moments. Some sang out they are our men — some they are all indians. Col. Foster cried out to a volunteer, "What the Devil you at there don't you see they are our men." They approached quite near (100 yds. some of them) & kept up a fire for an hour & a half or 2 hours. They hit one man — hurt nobody. Then they retired to just about out of gunshot range and rested letting off a stray shot now & then. Ah — they did not retire till it commenced raining, pouring hard. They kept up a continual whooping but the rain did not drive them away. I thought their spies had discovered some[one] approaching us which it was their intention to stop. At dark they made a fire less than half a mile north of us — if those who are dressed like soldiers should stand up round it an express to us would run directly to them. Our fires burnt all night. There was no firing at reveille.

4th. Immediately after reveille we sent out some men to get wood. They went about 100 yards off & proceed to cut down two "candles".[51] Before the trees fell the woods all round them were illuminated by the flash of Indian muskets & rifles. The men came rushing tumbling in, heels over head, over the breast work like a flock of sheep over a bridge railing. Not one was touched. Last night was a dreadful night — cold & rainy. Today it is pleasant. All the corn, public & private is collected (a mighty small quantity) to be henceforth refused to horses & given to men. The provisions are giving out. Lt. Duncan[52] and myself went to see the river. At 9 there was a general inspection. In (B 4th) there are 1300 cartridges, good. During inspection the enemy kept up a small fire upon the camp and one of them blew a fish horn "tut—tut—tut—tut". I hear that some of the volunteers have been round picking up the scattering grains of corn left where the horses have been fed.

The Eastu Charties[53] are all round us all the time & as saucy as we might be if we had something to eat! 36 (I counted them as they passed round from it) entered the hammock on the Infy. left — discharged their guns at the Sentinel without stopping to aim — and made a straight shirt—tail out of it again for fear of the 6 pdr. Lt. Mitchel my caterer says that we can have no dinner today — i.e., we can't have dinner and supper too — So accepted Whiting's invite to dine with himself, Linnard, Henderson[54] & Major Belton.[55] At this moment (abt. 3 o'c) the Seminoles are firing their rifles on the right 4 or 500 yds off as if they were hotly engaged there. Then! a rifle & a howl on the left — pop! it goes on the right again. There a musket on the right, the bullet half dead flops over my tent — there's a rifle on the left again! All is quiet — the soldiers cooking — chatting & laughing round their fires occasionally making some broad jest about the yell of the savage or the whistle of the "blue (rifle on the right) pill" as it is flying far over their heads (another), (another). I am sketching a plan of the camp. My compy. being out of bread (there's a musket from one of our volunteers — & a rifle! I'll bet they didn't either of them hit anything — the rifle I hear them saying was from one of our friendly Indians), Genl. Gaines has (rifle on the right) given me an order for some of the (volunteer musket) corn (rifle on right) collected today — a pint for each man. I have given them directions to boil it — not parch it — because it will go further — (volunteer musket on the right). It is no kind of use to fire at such a distance. Ah, that's right! I hear an officers voice telling them to stop it. In one hour every face will be turned in one direction & cast searching glances between the trees for the approach of an escort & provisions.

The friendly indians in our camp heard Powels speech in the night of 1st. He said "We can't do anything with them here boys but we'll give it to them when they come over the river!"

Sunset. A few are in the hammock on the left. Their shots come straight & swift. The Col. thought the citadel perfectly defiled [but] these shots have discovered an opening to it. The fellows have the coup d'oeil[56] to show us the faults of our works.

Dusk. The Indians are popping away right & left squealing & shooting. A report has just started that a drum was just heard to the North East as if beating retreat. The Indians appear to have divided since morning into small parties — I do not think the half of them has been here since 7 o'clk.

I was waked by the smacking of the lips of war twice during the night — It was a very cold, dewy bright moonlight night.

5th. I was up an hour before reveille — all was perfectly still. Save now & then the neighing of some hungry horse not a sound was heard but the snoring of men around me. The silence to me was awful portentious. At reveille there is not a pop. The ground is covered with fog & smoke, men stand around their fires, 15 minutes expires — one rifle is heard, a moment after one hundred and the bullets twitter over our heads like a rush of blackbirds on a fine morning. Under cover of the mist they crept closer to the lines with the hope of hitting some of the heads that were huddled round the fire. They fired two rounds each, howled & drew off a couple of hundred yards.

Sunrise. All is quiet. A single indian whooping on the left. Half an hour. Two or three are certainly very near the front — I'll go & look out. Went to see Gen. Gaines.

12 M. The Indians at long gunshot distance say 1/2 mile off have continued firing without cessation at the average rate of 5 or 7 shots pr. minute. I understand that a volunteer named Butler who was out cutting wood was shot through the head the ball entering the eye. Another wounded in the arm. At 1 1/2 o'c the firing ceased for two hours. During this time Lt. Izard was buried in the Bastion, 7 paces south of a beautiful live oak which spreads its branches over the grave. He was "No useless coffin enclosed his breast" wrapped in a soldiers blanket and was laid as a soldier lies down to temporary sleep. There was no ceremony that the enemies spies could observe.

I am sick at my stomach the whole camp is scented by the carcass of a horse decaying outside the lines unburied. A horse has been killed today & cut up into beef — a part of him is cooking at every fire! Several officers I perceive are having some part of him served up in their messes. Horse head soup is spoken of in some praise & in actual preparation.

At 3 1/2 the fire recommenced as if the enemy had finished his dinner & picked his teeth i.e., in a manner rather careless, sleepy and business like as if it was a thing that they must do & they didn't care how it was done — a voley once in half an hour & a single gun once a minute. Sun 3/4 hour high. PM. About 100 are seen northeast running with all their might to the left in single file. They fire. It cannot be ascertained whether they fire towards or from us. We hope they see the provisions & guard coming! 10 minutes have elapsed. Now they are firing at us. I lay in my tent here — my company is before me peeping through the loop holes with positive orders not to fire & certainty of punishment should they disobey, unless they kill an indian. Their elbows itch to draw a trigger when they see a red man if he is a mile off. They are talking with all brogues on their tongues mostly Irish, Dutch, English & American. They say the Eastu Charties are going into hammock on the left to fire on the guard at gd. m[ountin]g. Now I must get up for the bugle gives the signal for me to march on as off. gd.

Sunset. They were in fact running round for fear they would be late at gd. mtg. One chap was bold enough to fire from the very edge of the hammock he was 100 yds from the gd. & fired through it without hitting anyone.

6 P.M. The impudent rascals have a cordon of fires entirely acrost our peninsula! 5 in no. Lt. Izard was probably promoted to a Captain of Dragoons. Before he died he thought so but no official information had reached him. He was (26) years old. A graduate at West Pt. ('26 or 7). He commanded the advanced guard on the [28th]. As it approached the hammock of the river it was fired upon by the Indians. He did not know it but it was merely a hammock in which the enemy was situated

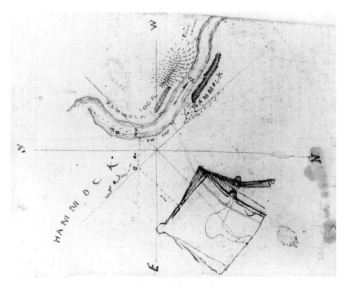

8. Camp/Fort Izard on the Withlacoochee River

& ordered to charge it through. The guard charged till it came to the river when a ball entered his eye & came out near the temple. He fell senseless on his face. When his conciousness returned he rolled over & told his men to "lay low & preserve their position." He then requested to be taken to the rear and was unable to speak after that day.

The horn was heard twice in the woods at between sunset & dark.

9 o'c. P.M. With the guard. All <u>blazes</u> in our camps have been extinguished. I have been snoosing on the ground for an hour. Waked by Lt. Linnard, Senior ofr. gd. tonight. The whole guard was paraded as indicating something extraordinary going on. I asked what the gd. was turned out for. The answer was "didn't you hear that conversation?" "No" said I. A negro voice in the woods called for Gen. Smith[57] — afterwards for Col. Twiggs. I heard him talk with Col. Twiggs — I couldn't understand all he said. I could hear him say that if (he wouldn't be hurt) "I'll come in the mornin, I'll come at one o'clk in the mornin sir." "Very well" in reply to Col. Twiggs & "Aye, aye Sir!" & "Good night sir." 1/2 an hour afterwards he returned. Said he would come "After breakfast tomorrow." Had something else to say which was understood that if we would allow no chopping tomorrow it would be considered a good peacable sign. He again said good night sir — & nothing more was heard from him. We are on the qui vive expecting some treachery — & all laugh at the idea of the negro's coming in. No firing at reveille. Buzzards & ravens hung in clouds on the other side — near the same place I heard foxes barking in the night.

Sunday 6th. Very pleasant. Everybody is talking about the probability of the negro's being sincere. And everybody sneers at the idea of his coming in. Yet they seem to think he may come — & that peace may be proposed. No chopping is allowed. We are perfectly prepared for the explosion of any kind of a plot that can enter into the imagination of the Eastu Charties.

7 1/2 o'clk a long string of indians or negroes say 100 are going slowly round to the right. All wrapped up in their blankets. They halt in rear of the pond & sit down in a circle.

Adjt. Barrow speaks to them; "What do you want? If you want anything come in. You shall not be hurt!" Adjt. B. at length takes a white flag on a ramrod & advances 20 paces from the breast work — mounts a stump & calls to the negro to "come on". To the utter astonishment of the whole camp, the negro comes — without his gun! But he came to a halt at 100 yrd. off — expresses doubt — making a gesture with his arms & hand, as much as to say "I know you" then walks back & joins party. At this moment a cry arose in our camp "there comes our looked for army." I looked & saw a long column of bayonetts glistening & even thought I saw the baggage waggons! A very few moments showed them to be indians coming in towards the fort from the right in number say 200. They halted and sat down near the other party. 5 minutes after[wards] a squad of 5 with their guns were discovered escorting a white flag to the right & a little in towards the camp. They sat down on a log. Three volunteers went up to them bearing white flag they shook hands & all took seats on the log — where they passed a half an hour. The volunteers on their return do not recollect the conversation perfectly. What they report is this. The firing yesterday was by the young men — they tried & couldn't restrain it. They do not want us to cross the river. Their main body stays there all the time. They will let us retire without molestation — if we attempt to cross they will fight till 1/2 their force is cut up. They say 6 companies are on their way here which they request us to have withdrawn. Capt. Hitchcock[58] has gone to see them — he will bring something correct. Capt. H. has told them all the preparations made by the U.S., guns, ammunition & men. That part of the army is expected here tonight. That we shall not move from here till the other forces arrive — and other <u>facts</u>. Capt. H. says he met Powel, Jumper,[59] Alligator[60] & Powell is a very interesting man, small, handsome, of a melancholy cast & a little talkative. Alluding to the death of Thompson he says he is satisfied & doesn't care what course is taken now by the rest of the Indians. Capt. H. is convinced that they are tired of the war & wish for peace. From some expression he does not recollect what it was he was perfectly convinced that they had not captured any part of our express. Jumper was spokesman. He states that they have 500 men on the other side besides Micanopi's band, not here, & 300 on this side. They agree to meet again when <u>the sun is lower</u> & come to a head — in the meantime there is to be no firing on either side. There is no limit to our <u>vigilance</u> however.

They are this moment (11[o'clock]) killing two fat dogs & cooking out a horse for beef. <u>Two </u>horses have been killed & served out in ra-

tions. A quarter of dog meat sold for 5$ — By George this looks like
peace! The men are all over the woods — the Indians look at them like
a tiger at his masters lamb. Capt. Hitchcock (sun 3 hours high PM) is
sitting on the log out there in conversation with Powel & other chiefs
— the Indian army is just in rear of them. I have watched them till my
eyes ache. Scotts compy. & mine are ordered to jump over the works
& fight them if they make any treacherous movement. The Indian army
moves off! Capt. H & the 2 that accompany him rise. They shake hands
with the Chiefs! The Chiefs move off. Capt H. goes from the Fort —
he runs — one of his companions turns this way, mounts a stump swings
his hat round three times with all his might. Capt H. walks this way.
They turn & go back — they stretch their necks as if looking into the
woods. At last all three are quickly returning to Camp. Mounted horsemen heave in sight! Troops behind them! Waggons! Packhorse! Droves
of cattle! It is with the greatest of difficulty men repress their joy from
breaking out in one loud shrill glorious welcome! They are ordered to
keep perfect silence on a/c of our relations with the Indians. For Capt.
H. reports that they have assented to <u>every proposition</u>! Oh! Bad!!
Our troops fire a voley at the Indians. They kill one. Heroickally [sic]
& true to their character — warrior like, they return the fire & give
their yell — (2 rifles) then stop. There is no more firing, our cavalcade
advanced. How grand they look! How I would delight to have the
world feel the succession of feelings — see the exciting panorama of
events, acts & pictures that I have seen, felt and experienced this day!
Moved my <u>boobyack.</u>[61] Slept soundly & sweetly.

7th. Have lost my handerchief! How perfectly quiet everything is.
The negro Abra[ha]m[62] from the other side of the river told the Offr.
Day in the night that he would come over in the morning and have a
talk. I have been walking on the very edge of the river an hour or
more. It is a dark, deep & beautiful stream about 40 yrds. wide.
Fringed with a thin hammock of live oaks intermingled with cypress
trees & scrub palmetto. The bank is clay nearly vertical & 5 feet above
the water. I saw no Indians. No doubt they were lying in the palmettos on the opposite side. The soldiers are forbidden to go towards it
for fear they will talk to the negroes & spoil the treaty for a soldier
was accosted there this morning by one — "Good moring sodjer —
how do you do this morning — how long are you going to stay here?"

The soldier said "I don't know — I wish that I was back to Georgia."

During the conversation yesterday, one negro stated the force on this side of the river to be 200 — another speaks up — 200! I guess you'd better count em — you'l find um 1, 2, 3, <u>400</u>. O yes, says the other, 400. They said they knew we were from a <u>foreign country</u> — and that we might return to Tampa the way we came but that they couldn't let us cross the river here. They wished to know if we were going to make a plantation here (where our camp is), said we might do so if we wanted to but must not cut the trees. Someone in camp commenced splitting wood. They said we must keep our young men from chopping during the consultation. Capt. Hitchcock sent in & caused it to be stopped.

Monday 7th. Evening. No Indian or negro has been seen or heard since morning & then only the negro I mentioned. The usual guard of 60 regulars (beside the volunteer guard, two separate commands) and the sentinels are directed to keep up the usual watchfulness. With this exception the camp presents the appearance of a time of peace. Our people go about the river & the woods without arms gathering wood & moss & looking at the bullet holes. Miccanopi is the supreme <u>civil</u> chief of the nation and is a Peas Creek.[63] It is difficult — I mean impossible to ascertain whether our enemy is removing the women & children to the <u>Wackasouci</u>[64] — or whether he is merely delaying to ascertain the sentiments and views of their "governor". There may be in the night, a voice from the other side to tell us that a white flag will come tomorrow & hold a talk. But if not, what our army will do but fall back onto Fort Drane I do not forsee. Such are its unfortunate circumstances with regard to provisions, ammunition & the orders touching it given out by Gen. Scott. If we had 10 days provisions & could keep the force that is here now, we could terminate the war whatever the armistice results in, but Gen. Scott calls our able skillful & gallant Genl. the <u>interloper.</u> And has ordered Genl. Clinch to refuse him assistance unless he is in a starving condition & then to serve him out but _____ days rations at a time — besides to take command of such part of Gen. G's force as was ordered into Florida by the Govt. (5 companies of Regulars).

8 o'clk. There is a fire on the other side. I have sent to Gen. Clinch's camp for a newspaper. Lt. Wilson[65] sends me a Boston Galaxy of Jany. 23. Quite a treat.

8th. Rainy. The Indians were not heard from in the night. It is now 60 hours that these woods have [been] silent & quiet. The boldness of the enemy and the howl which indicated a ferocity that could only be calmed by blood have sunk into the shyness of the wood pigeon & the stillness of satiety. We were not a little surprised at 9 o'ck. A.M. to hear the thunder of a cannon mingling with that of the sky. It was apparently about 4 miles distant in a Southerly direction and is supposed to be Col. Lindsey[66] from Tampa Bay. It was not replied to (on the supposition it was thunder). The body of a horse lies in the brook where he dropped down dead last night. A party commences sawing boards to cover the hospital. A command of mounted men are out foraging. The clouds break, it is the intention of the day to be pleasant. The army intends to hold its position & to expect the Indians all day today. The bodies of 2 Indians are out in the woods.

The proposal to the Indians amounts to this. That they shall go to Tampa & wait for <u>further</u> proposals, from the President. One article,

(the last) was about to be read to them as the troops hove in sight & stopped the talk. When the chopping was heard a negro rose & stretching out his arm said with authority "That chopping must be stopped!" Capt. H. says, "Capt. Marks have the chopping stopped". Capt. M. would like to flog the nigger. An officer from Gen. Gaines arrived in time to prevent a second discharge. Only the left flankers of the mounted men fired. It is stated today that no one was killed.

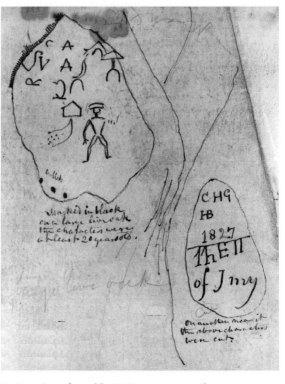

9. **Drawings found by Prince on two oak trees**

8th of March continued. It is now perfectly evident that the enemy has practice[d] with complete success a very often performed ruse de guerre. He is "hiepus che" — in other languages — gone away. Primus,[67] a negro, & 2 Indians have been sent over the river by Genl. Clinch as spies.

'in Camp Izard'   march 9th

10. In Camp/Fort Izard

9th. Pleasant. The two Indian spies of Genl. Clinch have returned. Primus has gone to the Indians. Billy says that Genl. C is "holy— wockerche"[68] for letting him go out of the camp. Genl. C. lectured the officers of the Florida volunteers. March on offr. gd. Rec'd. orders to take command of I Compy. Alvord takes command of (B). Transferred the necessary papers. Gen. Gaines turned over his brigade to Genl. Clinch and will go himself to N. Orleans. It is called in orders the "Light B[r]igad[e]" and will henceforth constitute a part of the Right Wing[69] of the Army in Florida. Retreat was beat this eveng. 1st time since we left Fort King. Tattoo also was beat in full.

10th. Rainy as usual when I am on gd. Orders to march in the direction of Fort Drane. All hands getting ready we start at 12 M. Thus, backs out a baffled army. Baffled not through want of numbers or the true spirit or a good leader — but for want of means & by the seduction of a subtle enemy.

Marched 6 or 7 miles — encamped on a very open place of rounded hills, dimpled ponds & grassy ground. Mitchel's compy. being the next adjoining mine we have boobyack together for the night. Lost a good square chunk of tobacco. Obtained a few layers of climer [?]. Knee deep in water several times on the march. Men have nothing to eat.

11th. At Reveille. Primus has returned. Was sent back by the Indians. To say that they had 33 killed, large numbers wounded. That they were not inclined to fight. Their breadstuff is said to be exhausted. They have plenty of cattle. They do not wish to go to the Mississippi. They were between 30 & 40 miles from the river. Marched sun 1/2 hour high. Reported last evening that the men have nothing to eat. Some beef was killed this morning — the men put it raw into their knapsacks — they roasted some of the tripe & eat it. We marched 3 1/2 hours & halted — fires were made & the beef cooked. At sundown arrived at our destination. 6 miles from Fort Drane. Our march had been very rapid & very fatiguing. Soldiers tired out — many fell to the rear. At dark some carts came down from Ft. Drane with bread & pork. Some rum too for the men — Gracious! How they revive!

(Mem. the dirge at Dades Battleground was "Scots wha hae wi Wallace bled").[70] On Battles: 1st day one killed 6 wounded. Volunteers one soldier wounded Arty. Gens. Gaines & Smith were fired on while examining the fort at the commencement of the action.

[*The following entries for the 2nd, 3rd, 4th and 5th of March are evidently an afterthought inserted here by Prince.*]

2nd. Capt. Sandys attached to the friendly Indians. Capt. Armstrong of the Motto & Lt. Izard of the army & 5 men were wounded — 2 killed.

Capt. Armstrong was fighting on his own hook. He killed 3 Indians it is said & wounded the 4th when his fun was curtailed by a bullet. Express on horseback sent to Fort Drane for provisions & ammunition.

3rd. Sergt. Davis of the Arty. killed, 34 wounded.

3rd of March. Cold wind high morning overcast, only provisions on hand for one day.

4th. All our comfort last night was a little fire. It was so cold & rainy that no one slept.

5th. One volunteer wounded in the arm & one killed.

12th. Up at taps — very pleasant — quite used up with yesterday's march. Slept in B. Alvord's boobyack last night, the men of I Compy. were I thought too tired to work. Errected a handsome log breast-work all round camp. As it contains only the regulars it is not very large. All within appear to have lost much of the asperity of their countenance to have become quite good natured. Conversation is quite loud and the laugh in one quarter is replied to in another. Wrote to Loring. F. Wheeler sent a copy of Genl. Gaines order No. 7.

13th. Mitchell my messmate went to Lang Syne. Brought some tobacco, and the news that Genl. Scott with some troops was at that place was brought this eveg. by Col Twiggs. Our camp is Camp Smith.[71]

14th. Genl. Clinch removes the troops from his plantation into the woods where fuel can be obtained more handy — Capt. Graham[72] takes command of his company. Some Regulars under Col. Bankhead[73] arrive at Lang Syne.

Company inspection at Camp Smith. Visited the volunteers — they are encamped a mile from here on a beautiful place for Florida & a good plantation. Their shelters are on a hill. A pond stretches along the whole length of its base in which one of their number was drowned day before yesterday swimming for an alligator he had shot. Returned & bathed in a beautiful pond north of Camp Smith with Whiting & Duncan. It is reported this afternoon that we march for the Indians again on the 25!! Marched on Offr. Gard., B. Alvord sent off Gd. Major Zantzinger[74] O[fficer of the] D[ay]. Read Young's Night Thoughts[75] while sitting my watch out — violent pain in my right chest. Reeve commenced messing with us at supper — sleeps in our tent this evening. Maj. Lear[76] went off home.

15th. To my surprise there was no rain at all last night! The Artily Companies (Grason's,[77] Adams',[78] Linnard's & Morgan's[79]) are ordered from this pleasant & peacable place to Ft. Drane to their chagrin as they had just got settled down in comfortable wigwams. Comps. H &

I are temporarily consolidated — so are G & D all of the 4th Inf. Doct. Brown dined with us.

16th. The 4 arty comps went to Ft. Drane. D company (4th Inf) came to Camp Smith. Our comp is with 4th. Infy. unalloyed.

Visited Ft. Drane. Got some papers. Applied to Secy. War for Top[ographical]. Eng. Corps. Single Offr. Gd. commenced.

17th. A volunteer who was wounded on the 29th in his ankle died in the night — his wound was supposed to be a slight one. Primus went to Ouithl&c.[Withlacoochee]

18th. On fatigue duty — to make a road towards the Ouithlac&c — the squad consisted of 50 axes & spades commanded by Alvord — 150 volunteers under Col. Lawson[80] protected it. About 4 miles of road was completed. When we returned we found that Col. Twiggs had left Camp Smith for N. Orleans. The reason of his departure is supposed to be that Gen. Scott pronounces Brevet rank to take the precedence where of prior date. Now Lt. Col. T. is the Lt. Col. of the 4th Inf. but Lt. Col. Foster is a Major of 4th Inf. but his brevet is older than Lt. Col. Twiggs commission &, according to Gen. Scott, commands. Col. Twiggs was heard to say, on the 17th, that he would not be commanded by a brevet rank.

11. **Assumed to be the site of Camp Smith**

19th. Capt. Graham & Col. Foster have gone. It is said that they intend to wait at McIntoshes till the grande arme is ready to move. Our Regiment is now a mere skeleton but is neatly situated and alone. Here we have 8 companies & 10 officers, Bvt. Major Wilson,[81] Buchanan,[82] Scriven,[83] Alvord, Myers, Scott, Mitchell, Reeve, Jno Graham & Prince. I am for off. gd. this eveng. We amuse ourselves in reading such old newspapers as can be obtained at Fort Drane, telling yarns of Knights and Ladies of Northern & Southern Society, domestic & foreign, civilised and savage. Travels, autobiographies, incidents & puns are jumbled together so as to make our conversation resemble our messes, being constituted of a little of everything we can get. Variety for the latter & what is stilled [styled] <u>news</u> for the former we are habituated to dispensing with. (materials on hand)

20th. It is no easy performance to keep awake all night. Even employed on somethig exciting there is a difficulty in keeping one's head awake. But sitting over a smouldering fire in a sultry night in the midst of 20 or 30 pipes of the nazal organ sluggishly snoozing the punkin vine, a man's eyes may stay open but his brain will sleep.

What with the unmitigated music of the toads & lizards — the baying of foxes & howling of wolves & all manner of sounds that the owls made — the night passed off tolerably quiet. It was only disturbed by one incident of apparent importance. The Sentinel No. 8 reported a great scampering of the horses in a direction opposite his post & that he heard voices. I dispatched a corporal & part of the guard with orders to bring in dead or alive any human being. He returned with his command bringing — nothing new.

Evening — Relieved. Relieved indeed. 12 o'clock at night. Called on Lt. Myers and after half an hours conversation we were frightened by the solemn approach of a procession with torches immediately thru. Camp. What was more surprising it silently proceeded to the shelter of Lt. Myers around which their lights were concertedly planted in the ground & left powder burning producing a brilliant illumination throwing the bark built shed into bold relief amidst the dark scenery of this savage time. Mr. Myers was very conspicuous in camp when he flew from light to light, his ghostlike figure beckoning back the dark.

Report of 2 guns heard in the night — supposed to be somebody fire-hunting.

21st. Rainy.

22nd. Gen. Clinch had 237 Regulars, 141 Geo. volunteers, 165 Floridians, 69 Indians. Courier came over, took dinner & Album[?]. Recd. orders to be in readiness to march in advance on Friday at sunrise. Appointed Adjutant of the Regiment. Events take a start & there will be food for journals.

23rd. Rode to Ft. Drane. The Dragoons under Capt. Wharton[84] arrived while I was there. A detachment was out after 3 indians said to be in the neighborhood — it brought in a fine large Deer but discovered no sign of a picus.[85] Dined with Lt. Linnard & Maj. Belton & [2 words indecipherable]. Whiting had gone to Ft. King. Buchanan intends to resign his little office in the big staff to exercise his big office in the little staff of the 4 Regt. This will force me to bid a long farewell to my shortlived greatness.

— There are some apprehensions afloat, for Primus has not returned, it is time that he was here now.

24th. Sent my morning report to Hd. Qs. by Reeve. Preparing to march. Camp is quite lively with military calls, business & circulation of orders. All the guns are discharging one at a time — to be cleaned & reloaded in 1st rate order. P.M. Lt. Buchanan arrives & takes his office which acquits me of Adjt. Duty & the pain of riding a hard horse on the march.

Report brought that Genl. Eustice[86] has with 1400 men including 600 horses fought 50 Indians at Volusia. It begins to rain — Horrible! I am off Gd. tonight. Mr. Simonton a citizen joined Capt. Graham's mess, he accompanies the army I believe as reporter for the Courier & Enquirer. Eat a stewed Goffer.[87]

25th. Rained all night. I accidentally knocked my shelter down about midnight & was obliged to take refuge with the men. It rains so hard that we do not move today. Two soldiers of Capt. Dranes compy. fought at Fort Drane today, one was killed. The rain ceased before noon.

26th. — The big day that so many have looked forward to, for which so much preparation has been made! How much has been said by the veteran few when smoking by a pitch pine fire about this day "when Gen. Scotts grand army comes to go to Withlacoochee!" The day is pleasant. The movement was commenced at Fort Drane about sunrise — their battalion was not fully under way till 8 — & the ground is so

saturated with water that a most horrible time was experienced in the
baggage train — our battalion fell in as the army came up to us, about
12 o'clock — several horses had given out & were left on the road.
They were at least 4 hours going the next 4 miles. Pack horses would
sink in up to their bellies. At dark we all got into camp — 10 miles
from Ft. Drane. On the road the Qr. Master gave me a letter from
Houghton[88] & Abba[89] — the first intelligence from home since I left it.
Great Appollo! How agreeably was my mind occupied all the rest of
the day. I could have marched to the Ouithlacoutchy & not known
that I was marching! Quarter hour after Tattoo we had an alarm —
the facts are: a waggon broke down 3 miles back containing 4 bbls.
flour — Knapsacks &c. 3 negroes & 1 or 2 white men (only one armed)
were by it when 7 rifles were discharged at them — one negro was
killed — one captured — & the alarm was started by the third coming
into camp. The Indians took 1/3 of the flour — scattered the rest on
the gnd., ripped the knapsacks, took the bread out & cleared, leaving
all the horses but one. The dead negro was brought into camp & buried. He was shot thro the heart — the live negro thro the clothes only,
in several places. The horsemen were out there nearly all night.

27th. Started early — had to bridge the road entirely till we got
onto the sand hills — we then found dry sand. Lt. Myers' company &
mine worked hard. I began to think when I saw the heavy waggons
stalling along that this was Genl. S' "faux pas." Encamped at our old
ground (coming up) — very tired — on guard with my whole <u>compy.</u>
I was amused at the Offr. Day "don't allow the woods to be set on fire
because it will burn the sentinels up, or drive them in" (the ground
was covered with thin grass).

28th. Made an early start. Saw Lt. Dancy's "works" — he was
perfectly safe. We aproached the river slowly on account of the
waggons. At 11 the head of column halted close up against old camp
Izard, about the same time a field piece was fired "for the fun of it" —
in other words to wake up the Eastu Charties, knowing that if they
were here they would yell or shoot at the voice of the great gun. We
harked — & then went on sad at the idea of their being gone. Some
said they knew the buggers were not here — some had guesed it before. One man said to me, fairly crowing over me, "Well <u>now</u> what is
your opinion as to whether the indians are here". Why said I that we

haven't reason enough to form an opinion. My compy. was marched
to the guard parade ground — it waited then till one o'clock for the
offr. Day to dispose of it — not many minutes from that time (30 min.
or less) old acquaintances sputtered out their venom off to the left of
the front. I did not hear any yell & think there was none. At 3 a log
breast work was commenced. No notice was taken of the firing except by a loud laugh of agreeable surprise. Our strength is 2070 men.

While the new guard was saluting us as we marched off, Indian
rifles were heard, about the same number as before. A trail has been
opened to the river — preparation to cross in the morning early.

29th. No fog, but the sky is obscure. In the dark of the morning the
crossing was commenced by Capt. Robertson's compy. One of his men
(Graysons comp.) crossed 1st., swam the river without making any
noise, took the end of a twine in his mouth which he afterwards drew a
rope over with. <u>Their Star</u> Spangled banner (vide 22.d Feby) was tied
round his head — this he hung on the opposite bank. A <u>little after sun-
rise</u> my compy. is over & formed. I have wrote this much sitting on a
palmetto root on the west side of the Withlacoochee. As yet there is no
molestation. The troops are crossing very rapidly. The Indians fired &
whooped in the evening after dark — I was at the ferry on the other side
— we all immediately went into Camp Izard. The canon was fired twice.

9 o'clock P.M. All & everything is over now.

30th. Sunrise. The companies are ordered to cook their meat —
when it is cleverly in the pot — they are ordered to get ready to move
in two minutes — yesterday the 4th. moved without any previous notice. I conjecture we march to Genl. Clinchs battle ground. We m[ove]d
up the river past Gen. C's ground, saw a fresh trail, countermarched,
left the baggage & followed it — we caught up with their stragglers &
occasinally fired a shot — at length we came to an immense prairie.
On the opposite side to where we were we saw the indians — looking
at us! Some parleying — white flags — etc. till near sunset. We encamped on the margin of the prairie. Beautiful to the eye but tremendous bad for the feet & legs occasionally reaching to the middle.

31st. What a day. We started across the Praire. Left in front first
on the lead was Lt. Graham's company, next Reeves' & then mine.
There are Islands of hammock in the Praire impenatrable to day light.
Some officers on horse attempted but could not get along. I saw one

horse sink so that his face only was out of water. The men all crossed the place through — horses left behind. Emerging from the praire onto green oak scrub, the Indians fired out of scrub. We formed into line firing & shouting as we ran into the scrub — the whole army then advanced "in line" but all the fighting was between the 4th. Regt. & volunteers. The firing of the 4th. was spendid. The right flank of the line was then thrown forward and all advanced — through briar & bush & pond & praire & marsh till we came to swamp — cypress swamp. "O god who can describe that scene". Before we got to the Cypress swamp when in the midst of a scratchgrass pond, the grass higher than our heads — somebody said retire!

We enquired who the order came from — no answer. All to the left of my compy. broke off & retired — mine & those on the right of it by Maj. Graham's orders kept on through the swamp to the river. There we halted — found nobody on our right or left! We faced to right, marched 20 or 30 yds. & struck a beaten path — we followed this 1/2 mile over romantic ground then hove in sight of the rest of our regiment standing at "rest". Gen. Clinch had been requested to withdraw. "No", said he "not will the 4 Regt. comes out of that." After this we charged a tramendous hammock (of live oak, maple & magnolia, cane, etc.). On the right here was the bloodiest of the fight. We pursued the Indians on their trail which was red with fresh blood nearly a mile to the river. There we rested. During the rest, we heard three distant cannons in difft. directions. Coming out of this I passed two volunteers dead, a third dying, all shot in the head. Arrived on open ground, the army formed & rested, got in the dead & wounded & bore tham off on litters. I crossed a portion of the praire on the skeletons of cattle that had sunk there & died. We marched to our baggage — where Maj. Wilson looked pretty safe amidst block houses & breastwork. In the first charges (i.e. of the Cypress Swamp) a Dragoon was mortally wounded. One of Capt. Robertson's flankers saw an Indian following us back when we gave up the chase. In camp I followed 2 to the grave this evening.

April

1st. The first thing I did after I got up was to follow the poor Dragoon whom they were taking off in his comfortable blanket. The dying man (Roberson) is not yet out of his agony. He is shot in the head and much of his brain has exuded. We marched up the river & burnt two towns. Saw no Indians. Encamped by a large lake on our way to Big Swamp — distant cannons heard in the evening. Patioges[?].

2nd. Aroused at 4 o'clock to march & marched at 7! We had a series of lakes on our left for 4 or 5 miles. Our destination was changed — we are now for Tampa. We left Maj. Cooper[90] & 300 men to establish a post — while halting for this purpose rabits in abundance scampered about us. We suffered for water all the afternoon — men & all very tired & broke down — we could not halt till we found water — pushed on & just as the sun was setting discovered a beautiful sheet — near it a large log breastwork, double row of loop holes. We occupied it. Supposed it to be Lindsay's. Everything shows that he has had a fight. Indians have been digging for the buried in several places. They are as savage as ever. In my opinion now, all of them intend to fight. We are to march at 4 tomorrow. Trail leading out is towards Tampa — a trail of Indians in pursuit. There must have been a large body on Col. Lindsay. Very warm. Our loss the other day was 10 wounded, 3 killed.

3rd. Aroused at 4, got off the ground at 8. Our march was fatiguing — weather burning hot. I rode a little, encamped 9 1/2 miles from Chocachatti.[91] Tampa they say is 30 from here. Passed some good praire & hammock lands. Charged a hammock supposing it to contain Indians. Set Chocachatti & praire on fire. On gd. tonight. Rain is expected. We have not had a drop since 6th. It rained torrents from 1 to 3 o'clock.

4th. Aroused at 4. Marched off near 7. Myself & company in the advanced guard. Beautiful morning. Grew very warm towards noon. Our road passed over some large flat praires with low grass & hard soil — firm travelling. The columns looked splended on them! Gen. S[cott] it is said has lost two of his aides, V & T. Made a good smart march of 18 or 20 miles & encamped on an open pine barren side of 2 large ponds. Perhaps 15 miles from Tampa, perhaps more. We cut our road by a deep worn Indian trail, single path & too narrow for white people. Quantities of men are broken down.

5th. Aroused at 4. Marched near 6, day hot. Progress slow. Great difficulty shows itself amongst the horses as well as officers & privates. The wagons are crowded with the sick & broken down. Arrived within [?] miles of Tampa. Visitors came into camp from there in the evening, telling us what!? That Col. Lindsay arrived there last evening & Gen. Eustis this morning. Myers gave out, I am left in comd. of H & I. We encamped only 1 1/2 miles from the river without knowing it!

6th. Marched down the bay about 2 miles & fixed ourselves. Got a letter from N.W. Brooks.

7th. I went over to see the fort [Brooke].[92] Quite a comfortable place compared to a pine barren! Maj. Sands is arrested for striking an Ala. Volunteer. Paid Mitch 15$. New mess — joined Graham. Capt. G. having left.

8th. I went to the fort. Maj. Sands[93] trial was held & finished. Newcomb[94] made his defence. Saw Capt. McLarren.[95]

9th. Unwell. At even. marched on gd. with H & I (having 4 men to each relief!). A cutter arrived this morning bringing a Spaniard & his boat, arms & ammunitions from Charlotte Harbor — 10 escaped. He promises to guide the army to the women & children if for his life. He has smuggled supplies to the Indians. The Louisa[na]. V[olunteer]s are to march in the morning for C. Harbour.

10th. The Louis. Vs. finished embarking at 10 o'clock P.M. Went over river, obt. 49 [?] from Maj. Belton for 4th. Infy.

11th. Capt. Robertson's Compy. moved over to the 4th. Infy. side of Camp Georgia. The 4th is to go by water to the mouth of the Withlacoochee. A howitzer will be taken with which I am willing to be troubled. The friendly Indians embarked for the West — with evident reluctance — one made a farewell speech to his hereditary home. One who was not on board at evening said he would not go — the squaws laughed at us for not having succeeded against our foe. The most affecting thing of all is the disconsolate affliction of their dogs. When all the indians had gone on board they collected on the shore of the bay & all together, set up a most pitiful cry.

12th. The order about the 4th. Infy. is countermanded — it goes by land tomorrow in compy. with ___ compys. of Arty & [?] Richmond Blues   [an inch-long blank space in text]   about 700 men. The 4 comps. of 2nd. Arty. that have composed a part of the force I have been with since the 26th of Feby. have left us. They crossed the ferry today & joined Col. Lindsay. This separates Whiting & myself who left N. York together in the most unexpected manner & by singular coincidence have been kept together so far — I regret parting with him. ... [*Approximately two lines of text are unreadable due to water damage.*] Well, we may meet — [?] — we may meet again. It is said that we march tomorrow. There is an appearance of rain. We have had but <u>one drop</u> since the day Camp Smith was disinhabited. The campaigne or tramp we are to commence is not expected to produce ill amongst our enemy — only against ourselves — dreadful marching sickness & the extreme of suffering is all I expect to see!

13th. Order for today is countermanded — for an order to march at daylight tomorrow — no rain. I have made my pay account for March & April including commg.[commanding] compy.[company] from 25 Feby. to 1st April $139.37 cts. & shall send them to [?] by Capt. McLarren. (Clark a soldier 5 ft. 5 in., light comp., sandy hair).[?]

14th. Marched at sunrise or after. With 4 Comp. Arty. & 8 of Inf. (? men). Geo[rgia]. horse & foot, offs. of 4th. Inf. (Foster, Wilson, Sands, Scriven, Buchanan, Jno Graham, Scott, Alvord, Prince). There are no less than 400 sick men at Tampa Bay. The object of our march is a profound secret in the breast of Gen. Clinch.

15th. Continued the march. We were cooled & enabled to march by one or two tremendous showers at mid day.

16th. Continued the march. Saw a flock of Deer — past some shady spots of prodigious good looks! Crossed the Prairie near an indian town where is some good land. Enc[ampe]d. on the north side of the prairie with a good indian hammock on each side of us.

17th. Continued the march. Rested ourselves & watered in Camp Chisholm. The indians had been there since we left it. A trail of 200 ind. reported ahead (it amounted to 700 before it got to the rear). Found 20 head of cattle at Cp. Chisholm, encamped near some indian houses. Took their cattle pens to put ours in. On Guard. I am the only Of. [of the] Gd. with 4 comps. of 4th Inf. Capt. Wharton O.D. — he's a bean — a f___. 3 horses dead this day. 4 left.

18th. Maj. Cooper's camp is but 2 or 2 1/2 miles from here. Some horsemen are sent forward. They see 40 indians. 2 horsemen returned wounded. There is a battalion sent to cover a horse. At 4 o'ck Maj. Coopers command arrived in our camp. An attack is expected tonight. I constructed a blockhouse for a gd. that will relieve mine. All fires are put out and all hand are tired so that we literally "lay low & keep dark".

19th. Early burned all our tents but one to a compy., broke our pottery after catching our cattle, [moved] on by countermarch for the point where the Tampa road intersects the Withlacoochee. Afternoon struck the river, marched along it 3 or 4 miles & camped on the bank.

20th. Cattle loose again. Fine cattle. Genl. Clinch lost his sword, Gen Powel[96] got it — name on blade. Heard Lindsays gun between 10 & 11. Replied to it immediately — arrived 4 pm at his camp on Tampa road. Gen. Eustis & his wing with Gen. Scott passed here this morning for Ft. Drane.

21st. Alabama regt. left here at 6 A.M. to scout the forks. Returned at 1/2 past 3 P.M. Gen. Clinch left also this morning with the Georgia Blues.

22nd. Made an early start for Tampa on the Federal Road.[97] Made a good march of 18 miles. I am on gd. tonight rested 2 1/2 hours at midday. Encamped between 4 & 5 camp Foster.[98] We passed two breastworks, occupied the third. Passed by time in the night walking back & forth on the last tracks of Henderson & Keais! I touched this road but once before & then a tear rolled from my eyes.

23rd. We arrived at the Hillsborough & forded at the Fort Alabama[99] near where the bridge was — the piles were burned to the water's edge. Being with the advanced guard I flushed a great many partridges during the forenoon. The gd. were reluctant to wet themselves. Lt. Scriven & myself waded & made them follow. (Camps corn & bacon).

24th. Made a good march of 19 miles to Tampa leaving the Alabama volunteers 2 miles out. The force that marched in was the remnant of the Light Brigade of bright memory — wanting the Louisiana Volunteers. No news at Tampa — not a word from the Louisiana Volunteers since they left for Charlotte harbor. Camped out of the pickets on the right.

25th. Polished myself a little! Graham went to the pickets very sick. Saw Whiting this evening.

26th. Started at Sunrise for Ft. Alabama joined by the Ala. Volunteers 4 miles out from Tampa (passed the grave of one of Eustis' men — it was opened partly & pries[?] under the legs — a broken [?] was lying by — the earth was damp.) Arrived before sunset at Ft. Alabama. Some Indians linger about here. Yesterday morning the first man that went out of the door of the Fort was shot with 3 bullets, 20 steps from the egress! Three men missing.

27th. Made a pile of barrels of Pork & flour & boxes of soap & candles that we are unable to take and burned them up. One of the missing came in this morning. We suppose the other two must have been taken by the enemy. Before leaving the Fort, one of the garrison fixed a musket & a barrel of powder in the magazine, so connected with the door that when the latter is opened the magazine will be blown up. At nine o'clock we took up the line of march for Tampa, discussing the merits of the "Infernal Machine."

At <u>ten</u> to our great merriment, we heard the thunder & felt the trembling of the blow up.[100] The whole army burst into a laugh that must have been heard at Fort Ala. At 2 1/2 o'clk while on a level plain partly surrounded by a hammock many had collected round the mangled body of one of the missing men — between one & two hundred indians & negroes commenced firing upon us. We stood their fire (occasionally returning their salute) for half an hour & then all being ready & the order understood the 4th. Infy. gave a tremendous shout & rushed forward simultaneously to the charge. They fired upon us till we arrived within 20 paces of the hammock. When we were <u>in,</u> the nature of the ground unfolded itself. Their position was behind a stout stream waist deep 10 yds. wide. Having driven them out of our way we left them to run their own gait. Coming out of the hammock we found the body of the other missing man. There were 16 wounded — 4 mortally. Our Column pushed on under the impression that we should have to fight them again in a large hammock one mile further. Arrived at this hammock, the 6 pdr. was fired into it twice before we entered. The indians in our rear mocked both discharges with a blunderbuss. It is at least a mile through this hammock. We marched several miles after we had passed through it. Mitchell very sick.

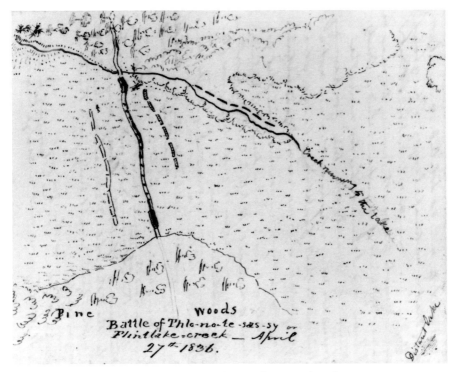

Battle of Thlo-no-te-sas-sy or Flintlake creek — April 27th 1836.

12. Battle of Thlo-no-te-sas-sy or Flintlake Creek — April 27th 1836

28th. Did not hurry from our ground. The sun was two hours high when we left our encampment. At one o'clock we arrived at Tampa. I find that Whiting left yesterday morning for Mobile, N. Orleans, thence North. There has been an arrival from N. Orleans but I can neither find a paper or hear any news. Several military funerals today.

29th. Unwell — took no medicine. Paid Jno. Graham 15$.

30th. Better. Doct. Nourse[101] dined with me on Turtle Soup. Hope of getting to Key West — blasted. Took (H) compy. Supped with Alvord's mess. The Louisiana Volunteers came across the Hillsborough & encamped beside of us. Storm Showers — Muster day. Assigned to Command (H) Compy. [?]

May

1st. No sleep last night on a/c of the fleas & wet blankets. I went out of my tent took off my clothes rag by rag & shook them thoroughly. The moon was in eclipse at the time! No sooner had I donned the articles of my toilet again than the rascals were taken by a stampede & raced up & down the hollow of my back & legs of my trousers in the most tearing style! Long heavy rain storm. Major Sands commands the Regt. I am A[sst]. Adj.

2nd. Slept out of my tent on a bench. Any place being more comfortable than a soaking wet flea hole. About ten last evening I was at the pickets. Saw a mule in the trou de loup[102] transfixed on a stake. His weight was supported by the stake penetrating the right side, his head was doubled back onto the left. A picture of agony. Lt. Alvord with (B) compy. embarked for Key West.

3rd. Set up most of the night & slept on the bench. Went to the woods as protecting party to workmen getting logs. Heavy shower — got wet through. After Tattoo at a meeting of the officers composed of Maj. Wilson, Dr. Lawson, Newcomb, Morris, Casey,[103] Buchanan, Adams, Duncan, Linnard, Tibbatts,[104] Ward,[105] Cuyler.[106] Intended that we should meet when there were officers of the 3d. art. present, but the opportunity having passed it was thought best to meet while there would be officers of the 4th. Infy. & 2n. Arty. The object being to take preparatory measures towards marking the spot contested with life by the band under Maj. Dade. The meeting appointed a committee. (Casey, Adams & Duncan of 2nd. Arty. & Newcomb & Prince of the 4th. Infy.) to recommend the proper measures of some [?] meeting.

4th. The rain this forenoon is very slight — wrote to Houghton. Sails are in sight coming up! Arrived. Rev[enue] Cutter Jackson, Hunter [is] Capt. Newcomb departed from amongst us.

5th. Hunter sailed — Steamboat arrived. Merely [threatened?] with rain, the shower passed by. It is said that there were no less than 3 horses in the trou de loup, commonly called gofer holes, last evening. I was passing Maj. Wilson's tent about 11 this evening when a dog happended to shout. The Maj. sang out from under the bed clothes, "Orderly — Orderly! take the horse out of the goffer holes".

There seems to have been a useless sacrafice [sic] of labour here — besides digging these "goffer holes" — the best orange trees were cut down — all the figs as well as the bananas. A person would almost think the enemy had been here — the spoiler has surely.

6th. The comps. (A, I & D) bound to N. Orleans (perhaps to Texas), have drawn off from us & do no more duty here. A most violent storm passed each side of us — we had a gale of wind that liked to have blown our tents over & a little sprinkle amidst bright sunshine — from sunset it commenced raining here however & in the night rained harder than I ever knew it to before. Paid mess bill 1 dollar & 6 bits.

7th. The comps. for N. Orleans embarked — a pouring shower — relieved from Adjt. duty there being no longer necesity for more than one. Tibbatts obtains a sick leave of two months from the time he leaves the post. The troops on board the boat fired their guns in the evening. Paper handed round as substitute.

8th. Worked all day at the blockhouse on the mound. Commenced messing. Profusion of rain from 12 at night till 4 A.M. Pleasant at 5 A.M. on the 9th. Camp removed to the Center where all encamped together. Relieved at night from further concern with the blockhouse. Steamboat sailed.

9th. Detailed to command the guard covering the working party in the woods. Went out in the woods, extended my men — put out pickets — & went to sleep. P.M. marched on guard — borrowed Duncan's hammock.

10th. As I swung in my hammock — witnessed the solemn burial of a soldier.

13. Burial Procession

A steamboat arrived to take the Alaba. people home. This arrival seemed to gratify everybody.

11th. At reveille every soul not specially excused goes out on fatigue cutting down bushes in front of camp. There will be no enticement for indians to come here by & by. Steamboat sailed. A great many soldiers drunk — mystery where they got the liquor. Mystery solved — a schooner arrived.

12th. Heavy rain in the night — out cutting bushes immediately after reveille. One vessel arrived in the night. A Captain came ashore with dispatches from the Governor to the Commanding Officer stating that the Indians are round about Tallahassee & St. Marks & requesting arms & ammunition. All the damage done might have been done by 7, I think as well as a hundred. They first made their appearance in that quarter 10 days ago. Marched on guard at 5 o'clock.

13th. A sentinel in the night was heard in a startling voice crying out, facing at the same time towards the bushes. Who goes there! Who goes there! Who goes <u>there</u>! Halt! Halt! Guard No. 6 — <u>Guard</u> No. 6! Guard number <u>Six</u>!! At the first call on the guard, I dispatched a corporal & file of men to see what was in the wind. The corporal & his men returned & lodged their arms — then coming up to me the corporal with great nonchalance threw out that "it was a cow, Sir, that frightened the sentl. on No. 6." A few moments after, I went to see the sentinel myself, thinking that peradventure it might not be a cow. He hailed me according to formula though a Marine, at the point of his bayonet I gave him the counter sign — as if he did not exactly understand he put his head & ears a little nearer & I pronounced more plainly the word "Virginia", which was the countersign. No — said he — shaking his head — throwing his gun onto his shoulder & turning from me as if he did not know precisely what to do. I started to approach him. He instantly slapped the barrel of his piece into his left hand & assumed the most unflinching attitude of a charge. "Don't move, said he, you'r my prisoner — for a few moments." I moved a little nearer & — "Click!" — flew back the hammerlock. I thought it best to stand and wait the result of a little reflection on his part. He held his gun carelessly in both hands, gradually eased off his attitude & took a look all round as if returning to his duty of keeping a sharp watch. Perceiving this disposition to neglect me — perhaps he might have forgotten that I was there — "Well, said I, what are you going to do about it?" "Silence, said he, I can't have any noise." "But don't you know your orders Sirra?" getting rather angry with him. "Silence" was my only answer. "Call for the Corporal of the guard Sir!" "Be quiet!" & this time he made a gesture with his gun as if to charge & assume an attitude again. "Call for the corporal of the guard Sir", instantly said I. "Silence" said he "I know my duty." Having given him the correct countersign — to be bothered in this way — I thought he must be drunk & was making preparations to hit him a shy knock on the bread basket with my weapon but determined to make one more effort to arrive at an adjustment & told him once more to call for the Corpl. gd. He sang out for the Corpl. of the Guard — saying that he did it to oblige me — that he was not doing his duty. The corpl. came. He had been furnished with a wrong countersign! No sentinel on post had the true one! Of course I suffered no delay in giving out the right one. An indian seen at a distance by Linnard. Stafford being at some distance on the other side of the river was shot at by 4 indians — wounded in the shoulder. Lt. Ward volunteered to pursue them with 10 horsemen. Motto arrived.

14th. Ward returned at 3 o'clock this morning. Was unsuccessful in discovering the Indians. The centre redoubt was manned this eveng. which finishes all three of them — and of course we are "ready" — only want something to aim at. Rode out on road about 600 yards from the edge of the scrub — saw plain tracks of two indians where they came up & retired — one in the middle of the road — one on the side — also saw & drove off two strange indian dogs — they did not return. The arrival of the Motto gives little satisfaction in the way of letters & papers though the latter are getting numerous.

15th. Sunday. Extremely warm. Flies & Musquitoes very troublesome. Coming out from breakfast discovered the sun to be eclipsed. Surface about half obscured. A boat full of officers of the Navy dined with us.

16th. Garrison Court in session. Composed of Adams, Casey & Reeve — I marched on guard. Reeve was too sick to march off. Wrote to Augusta.

17th. False alarm last night — Sent[ine]l. on No. 4 fired. Ascertained to be cattle very harmlessly looking at the works.

Offr. Guard not compelled to stay at the guard tent all day.

18th. Marched off guard. General fatigue — idly employed in cutting little bushes under an over powering sun! All dogs ordered to be shot but one who is notorious in camp for choosing the company of officers — being always with some one of them. Sentl. fired in the evening at some cattle.

19th. Out in the bushes doing this —

[Prince refers to the sketch at the top of the next page.]

14. View of Tampa Bay from Ft. Brooke

while the working party is gathering and burning twigs! Some attempts made by 2 miscreants to set up an establishment in the bay for trading grog to soldiers & powder & lead to the Indians. They were told to be off, and that a hundred warm lashes would be the recompence of their next visit. Removed our dining room to a house with spacious piazza & large trees before it. Sat in this piazza during a tremendous rain storm while the thunder and the lightening bursted & the rain poured in laughable fury! The feeling of sublimity when its proper cause dwells long, alleviates itself in a serious exultation resembling internal laughter. No one could have failed to admire the scene which was before me, framed as it was by the lofty wide spread branches of the huge live oak. It was the broad bay reaching miles on either side of me, the flat picturesque land with which it was skirted leaving an apperture towards the ocean and the extent in the field of vision might be infinite! Two low points in the horizon stood aloof that the picture might be sublime even without the heightening accessories of sound & motion produced by the wild impetuous exertions of nature's most powerful armies — gravity and electricity! Think of the ear being full of thunder — the heart trembling while the eye, ranging over the grand oak trees whose branches seem to mingle with the fire tongued clouds — that wide magnificent bay whose island seems to sink into its bosom — then, leaps into the distance over the ocean whose surface vibrates beneath the falling shower — and loses itself in vastness of extent. I enjoy myself amidst the free forms of nature! There is no society so sweet to me as solitude & one. Yet, all that is natural I enjoy. The group I admire — men as well as trees, but I do not wish to have the woods too near me — nor the mass of mankind. Individuals I love and I cannot be too near the trunk of a shady oak tree nor have my friend too near my heart. I am not a misanthropist for I always laugh at a good puzzle, it makes me "good natured". See a man engaged in conversation that you are not interested in & I know of nothing more commical to titulate the eye with — nothing that affords more scope for the imagination. Brilliant grouping of planets in the evening. The moon, Jupiter [?] & Venus all huddled together about the Twins. [?] are not Texas & Florida twins, they are alike in nature and from heathen darkness are being <u>brought to light</u> — at the same time — and the same mother is laboring with both [?] Spaniards & indians have been the tenants of both. And may it not be that the splendid conclave was that their noble stars might sing joy to the Twins together!

"The stars sing for joy" —

Don't you think it was a singing meeting?

It was really not a singe—ing one.

(**19th May continued**) I witness this beautiful phenonmenon at 20' before 8. These planets were then about 30° in altitude and were arrange pretty much like this

15. **Star Formation**

20th. Policing the plain today — several showers. On guard this evening. Duncan kindly sat 2 or 3 hours with me at night — read "The Stranger". 30 men on guard dismissed all but 9 at reveille.

21st. Passed the day in a <u>torpor</u> — could not sleep for the flies & musquitoes — Linnard & Casey with the Star have gone to sail down the Bay — paid Benjamin 2.66.

22nd. Slept soundly — too soundly — did not hear reveilee in time

to get up. Maj. Wilson is angry Ward says. Strange that he should be angry. I sent him word that I overslept myself. What is there in that to be angry about? If I neglected my duty why does he not arrest me — God forbid that I should beg Maj. Wilson's pardon. Would that quiet my concience? I had rather be acquitted. Who gave him authority to pardon. Horrible stench of carrion arising from several horses condemned & shot on the 20th. Why did not the commanding officer order them to be buried.

23rd. Marched on guard.

24th. Afternoon. A schooner & Brig came in. The first with Capt. Sanders & goods from New York — the 2nd [with] government stores from New Orleans. Both devoid of letters, papers & intelligence of any sort. Casey & Linnard returned. Marched off guard.

25th. A girl died — daughter of one of the residents here.

26th. Capt. Sands' command packing up for Suwannee. Linnard on guard.

27th. A visit from two naval officers, to get Watson.[107] A brig in — Capt. Sands. Lts. Morris & Mitchell & Dr. Cushman embarked at 3 o'clock on board sch. _____ for St. Marks with G & E Co[mpanie]s — marched on guard — paid Ward 10$.

28th. Morning. Capt. Sands' transporter sailed. [Appointed] Member & Recorder of a Garrison Court martial — unimportant cases tried — better than being on a general courtm[artia]l at first. Afternoon heavy gale south wind, some rain — marched off guard.

29th. Absent from reveille this morng. Orderly Sergeant says he waked me up — rascal! Just as if I shouldn't have known something about it! Guns discharged this day at target. Obtained a better tent. A schooner arrived from St. Marks for corn & hay — the Captain is as deaf as a haddock, so I presume he has not heard anything new lately. The Governor's letter to Major Wilson seems to think the Creeks are rising.

The family have buried a little girl today — it seems to be very sickly amongst them — a place which appears to me perfectly healthy & where the army enjoys good health is to natives sickly!

30th. Morning. Watson returned from the mouth of the harbour. Brought me a bundle of letters from on board the sloop of war Concord. Capt. Bunce[108] obtained them from Alvord at Key West and as he passed put them on board the Concord. The bundle is a treat, it contains two letters from Houghton with postscripts from Abba & Sophia written before they heard from me at Ft. Drane — also a letter from Carter Johnstone (with additions by Judson & Martin), Scammon, all accompanied by one from Lt. Alvord containing the melancholy intelligence of the death of Dr. Nourse who was apparently in the best of health when he left here & to whom on a brief acquaintance I have felt strongly attracted. He died on the 19th inst.! Court m[artia]l reconvened.

31st. Wrote a letter to Martin. Poor D[r.] Nourse! His immage haunts me. He had escaped the dangers of the campaign, which he hazarded, & died of sickness immediately after! He volunteered to go with Major Dade in Dr. Gatlin's place if they would furnish him with a horse. But there was no Government horse that could be obtained for him. This slender circumstance withheld him from death on the 28th of Decr. to die, when he was beyond danger, on the following 19th of May!

> "Peace to the memory of the brave
> However they fall
> Fame will the Warrior's ashes love
> His deeds recall!"

Afternoon — I marched on guard, Linnard being asleep and absent from his post, behind the Adjutant. Of course he will go on tomorrow & it will be all the same thing. Commenced a letter in the night to Abba & Sophia.

June

1st. Slept in my tent from reveille to breakfast. A young man by the name of Stafford, whose father furnishes us with beef, died last night of _____ very unexpectedly to those who have seen him industriously at work very lately. He started with Major Dade as Interpreter, at 3$ a day. A negro arrived at Tampa afterwards who understood this language better. The negro was sent out and Stafford returned! Death was determined to have him! After I marched off guard I went Whortleberrying on horse—back, they are on the decay.

The mocking bird drove a crow into a tree & then perched himself on the top of the next one; at which the crow said "krr—krr—krr" —

the mocking bird imitated him exactly! The crow then began to caw, which the other did not attempt but struck up the quail, whip poor will, tree—toad, robin, blue jay, kill—deer, marsh—hen & many others in succession. Astonishing musical powers!

Mid pleasures & places though we may roam

Be it <u>ever</u> so homely, theres no place

like Tampa Bay!

2nd. Sent by way of N. Orleans a letter to Abba & S. — one to Kendrick — one to Martin. Evening quite dark — large fire looming up off to the Northwest — suddenly extinguished at 10 o'clock.

5th. Sick abed — vessel arrived from Mobile.

6th. Sick abed — arrival from N. Orleans with compy. clothing —

Lt. Tibbatts came in here — whole pen full of hogs caught in the night!

7th. Very weak — walk about. The citizens keep dying yet.

12th. Well. Tibbatts left for N. Orleans — wrote to Scamman. We sent by the same vessel & under his care a whole family of little orphans with a letter, signed by all the officers of this post, in their behalf to the mayor of N. Orleans. Judge Steele[109] wrote the letter. How startling the solemn music of a funeral is — breaking out at once on one who has had no warning! I was reading <u>Byron to his daughter</u>, at the conclusion of the III canto Child Harold this afternoon when a funeral procession commenced its march. The fife screamed its note of woe, the drum rattled & the soft hammer fell, all in an instant & brought me on my feet! There was a soldier buried yesterday also. I am not so well this afternoon — have a relapse of my complaint.

13th.

14th. Mr. Sumner, one of the S.C. volunteers who was shot in the thigh on the march from Volutia, died last night. He was buried today by the Regulars with military honors. All the officers & all the men of the command attended the funeral. The olderly sergeants served as pall—bearers. His brother has remained here to keep him company throughout his sickness. The brother is now sick & delirious — he did not look out of the window to see the procession even. When I went over to the Hospital the deceased was not in the coffin; he lay on a bedstead covered with a sheet & his sick brother lay on the next along side of it covered in a similar manner. At length the coffin arrived.

The body was carried by the sick man's bed when they placed it in the coffin. He, poor fellow, looked out — shuddered — & covered his head over with the bed clothes. His remains were deposited not far south of the Redout nearest the river. He was about 35 ys. old and a very respectable man — wealthy, patriotic & intelligent. Patriotism was not an ostentation with him — it was a feeling. It is said that he willed to a brother practising law in Ala. a large amount of property on the sole condition that he would return to his native state South Carolina & practice his profession at home. He suffered more than any other man in the campaign that I know of. Others have died on the field — none have lingered such a period of wretchedness. Those who regret his death (and who cannot feel the loss of an excellent member of a community) find little to console them or quiet their resentment in the reflection that he suffered by the hand of a lurking Indian — or perhaps a runaway negro! — they must turn to the fact that it was not by the hand of his personal enemy but the enemy of his country — the deadly foe to the helpless woman & child that he fell.

> "Peace to the memory of the brave,
> However they fall!
> Fame shall the warrior's ashes love,
> His deeds recall."

He was buried at 10 o'clock A.M. Afternoon. I marched on guard. A sense of duty compelled me — not because I have got as well as the other officers but because they are all getting as sick as I am.

15th. Marched off guard. Passed a pretty heavy night — sleepy even unto faintness — but kept awake.

16th. I was absent from reveille this morning — the musick could not wake me.

17th. The brother to Sumners who died on the 14th, was also buried to day. He remained (though a man of 30) with brotherly friendship by the side of his wounded brother — his only friend in a rude place — his only comfort where there are no comforts or comforters till he died, & then dies with him.

19th. Marched on guard.

20th. Marched off.

21st. Casey & Linnard, who went to the Rancho[110] 6 days ago returned this moring at 9 o'c. They brought Purser Wilson & Lt. Ellison of the Concord who intend to stay several days. They were but 4 hours & a half coming up.

22nd. The Motto arrived from Pensacola with a most revolting great bundle of old newspapers. Whiting engaged on a railroad near Pensa[col]a — do not understand why he did not write! Confound him! Any more than I understnd why he has deferred this happiness of seing the north!! All the sheds for the officer's tents are completed — all are under them but myself. Wrote to Lt. Alvord, to go by the Motto tomorrow.

26th. Marched on guard. Duncan with a party of 12 (mounted) went out seeking indians yesterday morning at two o'clock, in the direction of a smoke scan the evening previous. Discovered no sign of an indian.

27th. Marched off guard. Ward & Waldron went to Indian River & returned.

29th. Morning. A sail in sight over the Island! — now for a letter!! Poh! It is Capt. Bunce from St. Marks.

30th. A schooner from N. Orleans is below. Lts. Duncan & Waldron & myself manned the barge & started to board her (a little before sunset). We had six good oarsmen & about dark we met a boat coming from her. Dr. Lee jumped into the barge from the sch[ooner]'s boat & we turned about — he says the vessel is ten miles from where we met the boat. I reced. a letter from Ed[war]d Pilsbury (at N.O.) & two papers — a letter from the QM General & from Major Glassel.[111]

Two northerners, Whitington & Suasy are passengers — the latter is a Bangorean[112] — the Brig is bound to Thomaston (Me) when she lands here some hay & corn. Judge Steele recd. a large stuffed leathern bag yclepped a mail — I may have some letters there, but cannot ascertain till morning. This afternoon Linnard, Dr. Reynolds[113] and myself rode out about a mile, went across the woods another mile to a second road — then took that road in, (a mile further). We did not see <u>a sign</u> of an indian.

The Captain of the Sch. & his two passengers are lo[d]ged on blankets in the mess room. Dr. Lee brings the news of Col. Foster & the three companies that went from here to Baton Rouge are ordered to St. Marks (instead of Texas as I anticipated when they left — vide 4th or 5th May).

July

3rd. Linnard, Casey & myself with some mounted men of the line —went out a mile or more & drove down the scrub for Deer — started three — failed to get one for want of dogs. We returned to camp, left Casey took Reeve & rode out to Dickson's plantation (6 miles) — found ripe tomata & water mellons & large green peaches. Returning saw the track of an Indian spy near camp — made this morning. Marched on guard.

4th. Very Quiet — Salute morning noon & night. We sat a little longer than usual at table and the following toast was sent in from mess no 2 "The day we celebrate & the cause we are engaged in — May they never meet again!" Marched off gd. Motto from Key West in sight below at sunset.

5th. Two letters from Alvord — accompanied by a box of cigars. Dr. Reynolds obtained a furlough for 60 days — he embarked this afternoon in the Brig Z_____ for Martha's Vineyard. I wrote by him to Brother Houghton — (10$) — paid mess bill 25$, Sanders' 20$.

6th. Motto sailed for Indian Key via Key West.

16. Fort Brooke, Tampa Bay

Lost some previous leaves

August

5th. Received my pay from 1st to 31 July 1836 — 74.50 — James
Light 5.9, Blue eyes, Brown hair[?]. Recd. from Lt. Ward for H Compy.
4 Inf. its share of the post fund 39.90 cts — paid my mess bill 23.87 cts
— paid Lt. Reeve 7.50 cts. The Motto from Key West & a Schr. from
N. Orleans arrived. They bring numerous letters & papers. Of course
after hearing nothing of what is going on out side of Tampa Bay for so
long a great many changes, of gloomy as well as cheerful caste, have
come suddenly to light. It seems as if they happened at the same moment rupturing the calm with gloom & flash. Who anticipated the
death of our late comrade Lt. J. E. Henderson! How unthought of the
fact that I have a niece! Yet the newspapers bear the melancholy words
& a private letter from home the pleasing intelligence. This is but an
instance — there is a crowd of them. We are in reality overwhelmed
by the rapidity of transitions in the progress of events. Poor Henderson
is dead!

6th. I have written to Sarah Parker Houghton. — Sent away my
pay acct for August $64.50 (not charging for commanding because I
may not command).

7th. Some Spaniards from Bunce's Rancho have come to tell us
that some of the hostile indians have been at the Rancho from whom
they learned that there was an attack planned on this place which would
take place tonight. O that it were true! We have no Generals or
superan{n}uated Captains to interfere & favor the enemy by their im-
becility & absurdities.

———————————

Mem. One great fault in the conduct of the late campaign was the
contemptuous neglect of known information. The indians at Tampa
Bay told the situation of the three bodies of hostile women & children
(one at Ocklawaha, one on a little river beyond Pease creek & one on
the Withlacoochee toward the mouth). Gen. Eustis went near
Ocklawaha & was attacked but passed on — leaving them firing at his
rear. Gen. Scott went within 3 miles of the party on the Withlacoochee
& was attacked. The Indians said over & over again that Peas Creek
was deserted (& in all these facts the indian prisioners, who had no

intercourse with any other indians, made precisely the same statement) — yet Gen. Smith was sent to Pease Creek — & he found it deserted.

Gen. Scott states in one of his reports that Gen. Gaines took all the means of transportation from Tampa which was destined for the central division of his army. Which was not the case for all the transportation Col. Lindsay had was brought here for the use of Gen. Gaines & arrived too late, as he had marched from Ft. Brooke. So much for prejudice.

Major Gates,[114] lately dismissed by recommendation of Gen Scott, some time ago told Lieut. Mackensie[115] that Gen. S. had never been a friend to him since he (G.) beat the Gen. at chess.

The following will illustrate the Gens. manner of playing. Lieut. Vinton[116] put his queen in check to which the Gen. paid no attention: Next move Vinton took it. "Not at all sir! Not at all! By no means sir!" — replacing the pieces — "Interest of the game Sir! Take the queen by an oversight! Clearly an oversight Sir — no man would leave his queen in that situation!" But when his adversary happened to remonstrate in this manner against his taking a queen — "Certainly sir — most asuredly — I shall take it! The laws of the game demand it if you leave your self exposed in so important a point." (From Lt. Adams — who was a witness).

Meeting Paymaster Randall[117] at N. Orleans: "Col. Will you play a game of chess — I see no other method of passing the time." "I will with pleasure." After the men were all set the Gen. said "Col. do you play a first rate game?" "I play tolerably Gen, I can't flatter myself that I play a first rate game." "Then Sir I must decline playing with you!" — and he left his seat. "Very well Gen." said Col. R[andall].

An arrival! Ho! A letter from Whiting. I see by the newspapers that I am promoted[118] & Graham promoted.

September.

1st. Majors Zantzinger & Mountfort[119] arrived — Rec'd letter from home dated July 3d.

3rd. — daybreak — alarmed by the report of a gun — it proved to be in the soldiers' quarters. A corporal of arty. He put the muzzle of his gun in his mouth & drew the trigger with his toe. Wrote to Plummer,[120] Scammon, DeForest,[121] Mother & Augusta.

Paid mess bill 19.60 — very cheap.

20th. The following permit was handed in for my signature "Private Jackson of H comp has permission to be 'married' to Miss Dixon, Fort Brooke E.F. &c". I signed it. Duncan broke his collarbone — horse ran away with him.

29th. Offr. Day. A report of a rifle loud & distinct was heard just as parade drum was going to beat — it was directly in front — a party of 20 horsemen under Lt. Adams sent out. He found Staffords house burning — the Indians had gone. Returned after dark.

Between 10 & 11 P.M. a barge arrived & brought Col. Lane,[122] Mr. Watson & interpreters. It appears that there is a steamboat in containing the company of arty. & 500 creeks!

30th. The Indians & troops landed. Between 100 & 200 of the former under Col. Lane & 20 mounted men from the garrison of Fort Brooke under Lt. Linnard went out in the afternoon. They found 30 or 40 Indians at Dixon's (7 miles). The creeks did not wish to meet them when they found they were coming to the reality! (O <u>Brag</u>!) So the mounted regulars rode in amongst them with Linnard & two were badly shot in the arm — also several horses. The fiendly indians not being allowed to return did their part of the holloring & firing but none of them have brought good proof that they were in reach of gun shot. The injury done the enemy is uncertain. One of the regulars rode side & side of a hostile indian on foot — he flashed his gun, the indian had none. While he was repriming a mounted indian near him disabled him with a bullet through his right forearm — his name Soda.

31st. Lt. J. Roberts[123] slept in my tent last night. The Creeks will start out tomorrow and if they don't get licked it will be because they have a few regulars with them! The Siminoles & niggers are decidedly the best fighters. Jumpers', Powels' or Alligators' band would whip the whole 500 Creeks. The news by the steamboat (of 30th) is both good & bad — Major Pierce[124] has had a battle near Fort Drane — Maj. Sands is dead — died on the Suwannee. Paid the mess bill 20.46.

October

1st. 1836 "O dear!" thought I when I waked up. "What can the matter be." To raise such a row — such a rumpus & a rioting. "Get my horse — my horse! A gun has fired! There's a buzzard in the air!

Death & salvation! Give me my horse! Dear me," said I, "Joe, what is the matter? Why [have] the Indians gone out & some guns have been heard? How long have they been gone?" "O about half an hour. They fired at a deer then of course." "Yes I expect so, but Capt _____ is callng for his horse which makes me think they intend to send us out"... so, Joe went out with his company & a handful of Creeks that did not happen to go in the morning early. After traveling 6 miles he over took the party & ascertained that they had not only killed a fine dear but a white crane. Nearly the whole five hundred Indians went out early this morning <u>without a white man</u> and "not to fight" Col Lane says. They took one of our old indian prisoners as a guide both being now out of chains. All the Creek Vols. but four or five returned in the P.M. — <u>they</u> are gong on to see if they cannot persuade the Seminoles to come in.

4th. Another Steamboat arrived — brings 250 Indians & Capt. Morris's compy. of arty. The Tennessee Volunteers are sposed to be at Fort Drane.

6th. At night the negociating party of Indians (4 or 5) came in & are very mysterious to the general questioner as to what they have seen & done.

7th. The negociating party have made their report. They travelled ____ days & came to Alligators headquarters — access to the place was extremely difficult being obliged to cross several streams. After stating the object of their mission (to offer terms) Alligator said that he had been fighting & fighting successfully and that he should continue to fight. He says the Indians lately flogged the Tennessee Volunteers & before they reached the Withlacoochee. He admires our mounted men <u>because they can run away so easy</u>. He told the negociating party that he saw them coming; he saw their large horses & thought they were white men with a flag, & that he made up his mind to hear what they had to say & then kill them. He says that a negro was lately sent amongst them on an errand from the whites and that he will not be allowed to return — they have him now & mean to keep him. He does not wish to spill red [Indian] blood but if the Creeks have made up their minds to fight let them come on. He told Bill (the loose prisoner who went as guide) that he should not see his wife or children — nor any of his kindred — that he was with the whites and might stay with

them. Bill said he was <u>caught</u>. Yes said Alligator, caught on purpose!
He wound up by saying that they might go & that he would be down
this way to accomodate us with a fight in ten days. He understood the
Creeks had come for negroes. We have plenty of them said he. Their
prophets & witches had said that the Great Spirit was on their side.
(Rem. I am wrong — the chief was not Alligator!) On the news being
received by the friendly Indians one of them made a speech in which
he said that they had come with the hope of making a reconciliation —
& had been unsuccesful — it becomes us now to act like brave men.
Some ofcrs. are ugly said he & some handsome — but after a battle
the ugliest man may be as handsome as anybody. I am very ugly (he is
very handsome in fact) said he but in battle you shall find me good
looking and — if I fall you shall say "there lies a brave man!" An
unfortunate accident occurred last evening in the camp of the friendly
Indians. One was accidentally shot in the head by another. The Doctors think he will recover. If he should not the unfortunate man who
held the gun, according to custom must die also. He will stand up still
& let them put a knife into him or shoot him. Indians have no horror
of death by either of these means — but they can't bear to be <u>weighed</u>
as they call being hung.

    8th. Wrote to Houghton.

    10th. Early in the morning Col. Lane's Regt. of Creeks struck their
tents and marched through our camp to the river. They did not finish
their crossing till most night. <u>Verrous nous!</u>[125]

    11th. Two Indians came in sick from the Creek Vols.

    12th. Two more. Duncan obtains a leave for 40 d[ay]s. Dr. Lee
sick. I sent to Major Mountfort 3 new publick blankets. Duncan left
in the evening.

    13th. Two more Indians. A sick Indian buried to day. His brother
was present. He could not cry, he said, his grief was inward. He paid
every attention to the corpse — put a new white turban on it — laid it
in its "narrow house" — put in his rifle — horn full of powder & all
his little trinkets & apparatus as well as a bag of corn. After the burial
he regretted that the white men did not fire over the grave & said that
as they did not do it <u>he would</u>. So he took his rifle, went to the grave
& fired three times. This man is quite anxious to get something to do.
He says he can't eat the white man's bread for nothing!

15th. A steamboat arrives (P.M.) full of troops — Gen. Jessup[126] and all. Now for a most glorious state of starvation at this post! The Indians are to be conquered in 6 weeks!!! GOD SPEED THE CAUSE! A letter — from Home, & some papers. Offr. Day this night.

16th. Major Churchill[127] came on shore, we shook hands very heartily — afterwards he took one of my hands & gave it a real thrible (sic) shake and said that he was directed so to do by my sisters. Gen. Jessup, Lts. Thomas,[128] Phelps,[129] Arvin,[130] Daniels[131] & others came on shore. All went on board again at night. It is probable that the troops will not land here — from this boat — prospect of speedy starvation consequently diminishes.

18th. Maj. Churchill assumes command of Fort Brooke. The Steamboat takes 3 comps. of arty. leaving one of arty. & one of Volunteers at this post.

19th. Doct. Lee left in a schr. for N. Orleans. Opened "box No. 27" — found 3 newspapers & a letter — from N. Orleans — marked "via St. Augustine". How did they get into a box of shoes from N. York?

23rd. Last night there was a voley of rifles & some screaming or yelling heard by the whole garrison. It occurred about two o'clk. It is feared that some express destined for this post has been cut off — perhaps from Col. Lane.

25th. The companies that went to the mouth of the Withlacoochee with Gen. Jessup — arrived here again in a Brig. Gen. J. has gone to Apalachicola. The command obtained no intelligence of Lane.

27th. Wrote to bror. Houghton. A steamboat in sight at 11 o'clk P.M.

28th. It is the steamboat Merchant with Gen. Jessup & the marines on board. It brings news of the Death of Col. Lane. Not by an Indian rifle — or by disease — but by his own sword. He passed his sword through his right eye into his brain on the 19th at Fort Drane. Heart—rending intelligence from the interior! Is the Great Spirit on the side of the Seminole? A youth of high promise has fallen — fallen! indeed! neither by the death breathing climate or the missle of his enemy! I am at a loss to conceive how [a] man like him could be led or driven to such a resource — to blast by that single blow the reputation [he] had established which formed the fairest groundwork of a life of usefulness & honor — to die by the stroke that annihilates all his career. O how deep — how dyed in misery — is the dismal glen of disappointment if this can be the cause!

In the course of the day the Marines landed. They are in good order and fully provided with comfortable tents.

30th. Col. Henderson[132] takes command of all the troops at this post. He outranks everything below the General.

31st. After muster went over the river com[mandin]g covering party. Gone all day. Rode out 3 or 4 miles, discovered no trace of Indians.

1st. Oct. caterer of the mess

"   "   paid to Davis[133] 5$

8   "   "   "   " 10$

16   "   Capt. Lyon[134] joined the mess

"   "   Major Churchill

"   "   Doct. McKnight

17   "   Received from Doct. Lee $11.25c

"   Doct. Bryon joined

"   Maj. McClintock[135] joined

"   Doct. Foray[136] joined

23   "   paid to Davis 10$

29   "   "   "   " 9$

28   "   Doct. Lawson joined

31st "   Resigned the caterership having served my month.

November

1st. Am transferred to K Comp., 4th Inf.

13th. Two hundred mounted have went to the Alaphia — found nothing.

15th. Passed recpts. with Lt. Reeve for compy property, dated 1st.

18th. Col. Stanton[137] arrived.

19th. Order to be in readiness to march at moments warning published.

20th. Paid Capt Sanders bill 53$. Mem. Ammunition — accounts

26th. Orders to march tomorrow morning out. Col. Foster (& Capts. Allen[138] & Morrison[139]) arrived with 92 Recruits of the 1st order all ready for the field last night.

27th. Col. Foster's troops landed. Capt. Allen takes command of

Comp. K. Col. F. assumes command of the Light Corps, I am adjt.

Gen. Jessup's army begins to cross the Hillsborough. The Infantry will cross tomorrow morning. Steamboat Merchant arrived bringing Qr. M[aste]r. Thomas[140] and a report that the Cove of the Withla. has been thoroughly scoured & that there are no indians there. It is a wonder that the army not be ordered back into old gtrs. again.

28th. Col. Henderson's Marines recross & Gen. Jessup calls for volunteers from the army to accompany him to Volusia. They are mounted & move off.

30th. Col. Foster's bat[talio]n. of 4th. Inf. & Maj. McClintock's[141] Arty. march for the Hillsboro. At evening encamp at Thonotosassa.[142] Alarm at night.

December.

1st. At 7 bury some 4th Inf. bones on the Battleground of last April — arrive at old Fort called Fort Alabama.

2nd. Am appointed Engineer to Col. Foster's Detachment of the Army of the South.

Commence the Fort.[143]

Finish the same.

17th. Received Command of Capt. Morrison's Detachment of Recruits 51 strong.

18th. Capt. Morrison left for Tampa

20th. Went to Tampa Bay

21st. Came out to the Fort again, met the whole Regt. of Tennessee Volunteers. The meanest rabble I ever beheld — they were stretched over 8 miles of the road. I thought I never should get by them.

22nd. Col. Foster with his Infy. started [north] to escort about 30 waggons of forage to Ft. Armstrong.[144] Four miles from the river met Gen. Jessup proceeding [south] to T. Bay. He immediately enquired if the bridge "at the Fort which he should call (when he arrived there) Fort Foster was complete." Encamped at Gen. Gaines' first breastwork 8 miles [south] from the Withlacoochee.

23rd. Arrived at Camp Eustis now called Camp Birch.[145] Reconnoitred the [Withlacoochee] river — unloaded the waggons. Express to Ft. Armstrong.

24th. Lt. Reeve returned to Fort Foster with the waggons & a guard of 25 men picked. Lieut. J. F. Lee[146] with waggons from Fort Armstrong arrived, took some corn and returned.

25th. Lt. Col. Freeman with a large force arrived as an escort to the waggons from Tampa. Lt. Reeve came.

26th. Col. Freeman with part of his train goes to Fort Armstrong. Three companies of arty. (150 men) arrive at this camp from Ft. Armstrong & report for duty.

27th. Col. Freeman returned from Ft. Armstrong. Doct. Wilson (who was at Camp Izzard) slept in my tent — he did not stop for coffee in the morning.

28th. Col. Freeman goes to Ft. Foster. The bridge across the Big Withlacoochee commenced under Capt. Allen.

29th. Talking of Col. Lane with Roberts. He says on the way — he [Lane] indicated distrust of the Creeks. Complained of his head, said one day that if he could only have half an hour's clear thought as he used to have he would give anything.

Bevins a soldier says that when Miccanope was abandoned last summer — Major Pierce ordered the compy. desk of D. Compy. to be burned without examining it & that a private soldier broke it open, took out my watch & sold it for 20$. ha! ha! ha! hurrah! hurrahh!

said one day that if he could only have
half an hour's clear thought as he used
to have he would give anything —

Bevins a soldier says that when Micanopy
was abandoned last summer — Major Pierce
ordered the Comps. Desk of D. Comps. to be burned
without examining it & that a private soldier
broke it open, took out my watch & sold it
for 20$. ha! ha! ha! — hurra! hurra!

January 1837

1   nothing
2   do
4 finished the bridge — the Fort is 4
5 & 6 logs advanced — Sin Boy arrived
last evening — bringing from the General
an order to march — when he comes
along.

17. Opening page of the Diary of Lt. Henry Prince for 1837

THE DIARY OF LT. HENRY PRINCE

1837

January

1st. Nothing.

2nd. do [ditto]

4th. Finished the bridge – the Fort [Dade] is 4, 5 & 6 logs advanced & Jim Boy[1] arrived last evening – bringing from the General an order to march – when he comes along.

5th. Visitors from Ft. Armstrong, R. W. Lee & Dr. Triples – accompanied them 2 ms. on their way back – so did Lt. Reeve.

6th. At 8 A.M. the General & his army appeared coming up the road. The whole encamps here. A letter from home & one from Scammon.

2nd Arty

4th ”

3d ”

Marines

Alabama Vols.

Georgia Vols.

Col. F[oster?]. arrested Capt. _____ after dark immediately after the discharge of both barrels of his gun inside his own tent slightly wounding Sergt. F. Introduced to [Bvt.] Major [James Duncan] Graham,[2] T. Engs.

P.M. The Gen. and mounted Marines proceeded to Ft. Armstrong. (To return tomorrow).

7th. An Expres from Tampa – the 6th Infy. has arrived there.

P.M. Gen. Jessup returned. We are waiting for the waggons to bring the stores from Ft. Armstrong to this Depot. Ft. A. is to be broken up.

Maj. Graham says the Gen. talks of letting him have about two comps. well mounted to examine the country — and wished to know if I would be willing to join him. The Gen. told him he would detail me — if I was willing. I accepted — & hope the corps will be organized by the General.

8th. Sent Returns of [Comp. G & Ordn] of K Compy. 4th Infy –

18. **Fort Foster on the Hillsborough River**

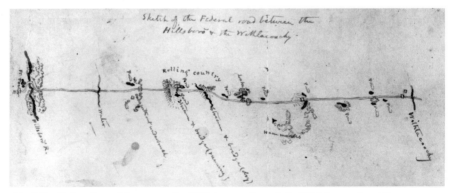

19. **The Federal road between the Hillsborough and the Withlacoochee Rivers (the Fort King Road)**

Also Invoices of some ordinance at Ft. Foster & Lt. Leib's[3] receipt for it. The Georgia & Ala. Vols. move on a few miles for better grazing. Organization of the Army completed this evening – the order is out – the main body advances to Fort Armstrong tomorrow. Col. Foster ordered not to move tomorrow. Fort [Dade] not quite done. A train has gone to T. Bay – Lt. Roberts & his company went with it. A train left this morning for Fort Foster.

9th. The train from Fort Foster returned.

10th. The whole Army except the garrison of Ft. Dade[4] (40 men & the sick) & the 4th. Infy. marched early for Ft. Armstrong. My d[eta]ch[men]t of 48 Recruits distributed & broken up. An express arrived this morning from Fort Armstrong bringing information that the Volunteers who left here the 8th took 16 indian & negro prisoners. The mounted volunters waste more than a pint of corn to every horse by leaving it on the ground when they move.

Evening. A train from Bl[ac]k Creek via Fort Drane proceeding to T. Bay arrived here commanded by Herbert.[5]

11th. Early arrived express from Gen. J. The Ala. have 35 more negroes amongst them Primus (Gen. Clinchs ambassador from camp Izard.) 150 mtd. Georgians coming on – ordered to march with their Col. F. in command (myself Actg. Brigd. Major) down the river on the south side.

Marched at 9 o'clk having waited for the mtd. men to breakfast & rest. Encamped at the old camp at which Gen. Clinch lost his sword last year. We marched 5 hours – the distance is 12 miles I think. Major Nelson[6] is a good soldier. At this camp we examined the ford & found signs of Indians & cattle going into the Wahoo Swamp – probably a week old or more.

12th. It rained all night. Out of camp by 7 o'clk. At nine the rain let up – at 10 o'c. the Col., Maj. Nelson, Lt. Searle[7] & myself with 120 men separated from the rest & moved ahead in hopes to reach camp Izard to night. At 11 A.M. came upon a small party of indians encamped & drying their clothing. Made dispositions for a charge but they turned out to be friendly Creeks. They had a poor half starved – half clad – Seminole prisoner (Tallassa) whom they took last night when the sun was about 2 hours high. At that time he could have got home by night to the camp of his tribe where he says there are many women and children & 250 men who have nothing to eat but Koonta[8] & beef without salt. They have but little powder which they bought of Capt. Bunce last winter (since they bought it the cold weather has come & gone). The powder which this individual had in his horn was a mixture of fine rifle & musket. His bullets were of his own manufacture, his rifle had a <u>wedge</u> for feather spring and was set off by pulling back the hammer & suddenly letting go the hold. His only garment was a shirt made of corn bags, probably picked up on our camp grounds last year. We made the indians pack up & join us – arrived at choco chatty 1/2 after 12. Kept on to Fort Cooper where we found an abundance of cattle & concluded to encamp which we did at 1/4 before 2 P.M. The rest of our force with the waggons came up at 1/2 past two.

13th. All marching at sunrise. At 2 o'clk the waggons & all were in <u>Gen. Scott's</u> pen (opposite Camp Izzard). We gathered today & yesterday at least a hundred head of cattle. A compy. of horse (25) went down the river to the ford & up towards Camp Izard on the other side to see if there were any traces of Gen. Jesup there. They discovered none but found fresh signs of indians (made today because it rained last night) in the hammock between this and the ford. The ford is a mile and a half down the river. (This accounts for the gun we heard just as we came in sight of the breastwork). Our horses being too much jaded we did not pursue. After sunset the cannon was discharged for a signal to the main army but we heard no response. Our men are ordered to sleep soundly till reville & lay in a good stock of rest.

We examined our prisr. this evening – he is quite intelligent and would tell everything apparently but our interpreter is a Creek who has not perfectly mastered the King's English. "His tribe bought their powder of <u>Captin Bunce</u> last winter for which they gave him Deer–skins. The camp to which he belongs is on Clear–water creek. It is composed of three villages inhabited by the Choceochutties, Euchees & Tallassees (250 men – <u>heap</u> of squaw & pickaninny). No negroes there – all gone towards the Wahoo swamp.[9] These tribes have but very little powder (almost none). He says he has a wife & one infant – that Powel has plenty of powder, that he had taken six kegs from white men in a fight this winter – the whitemen fought & then went back & were so scared that they left these kegs in the bushes – threw them away. He has caught fish for Capt. Bunce he says. When taken he was picking up corn in an encampment where horses had been fed – he beckoned to the Creeks first. He says that the hostile force here last winter when Gen. Gaines was here consisted of Miccasukees, Tallassees, Tope–Kay– ligays & Negroes. I asked him if Jumper was here – he said _no. Alligator? _yes. Micanopy? _no. Abram? _yes. How many in all? Don't know. How many Miccasukies? _300. Tallassees? 10. Negroes? Great many. How many Tope–kay–ligays? Dont know.

14th. Sunrise. Getting ready to march. This note was taken across the river by an indian who put it in his hand & swam over then put it in a split stick & planted it on the right bank near the crossing place.

"Camp Izard Jan 1837

General,

I am directed by Col. Foster to say that he has proceeded down to Fort Clinch.[10] His command waited on the opposite side from half past one yesterday till 8 this morning. A company of horse crossed the river at the ford below & marched up towards this camp to discover traces of your force. The 6 pdr. was discharged last evening between sunset & dark.

Very Respectfully
Your Ob. St.
H. Prince
Lt. 4 Inf & Act adjt.

We left Scott's "pen" at 8, our course NNW generally & over high rolling pine land. 7 or 8 miles from camp touched the river again. Losing the indian trail (which we found very straight) among the swamps of the river our prisoner volunteered his services as guide. We put him ahead & he struck a bee–line for the Fort Clinch & Tampa Bay trail which he reached in 4 miles. When near it he gave a leap & planted both feet in the trail facing toward the river. We encamped say 5 miles from Fort Clinch at 3 o'clock (& little after) to which place Lt. Searle kept on with his servant. We fired our gun at sunset. We caught 27 head of cattle today. In a hammock where we halted an hour or so today, I saw No–stee–Cha– pa–nee (our Sem. prisr.) running about with a joint of pork on his shoulder looking for his keeper!

15th. Soon arrived at Fort Clinch – joined by 7 comps. of the 4th.

Infy. and made arrangements for marching. Gen. Jessup arrived at Fort Clinch in the afternoon.

16th. Guided by our pris. directions we march for the camp of his people. Encamp 16 ms. south of Fort Clinch. Some signs [of] fresh tracks.

17th. Marched 4 ms. further & established Camp Lyon. Joined by Jim Boy in the afternoon with 80 creeks. Examined our prisoner more perfectly with a good interpreter. Jim Boy was present. The prisoner was melancholly & agitated. He said that the main camp or town was 3 ms. from the sea in a S.W. direction from this place, but that his wife & child were in a swamp three miles from here where there are 10 warriors only. The prisr. was told that he must conduct us to this last camp this night, his life depending upon it. He said he would not lie, he would show us the way but that it was very bad – and rivers to cross in the swamp. (mem[orandum] Tsa–wa–no–gay) At 7 P.M. the prisoner well wrapped up in blankets for he has a violent cold mounts a horse trembling with agitation. I pity him! We started for his camp with two comps. of horse & two of foot, he was placed ahead with a horseman on each side of him. After riding about 4 miles he halted at the skirt of a hammock and told the interpreter, pointing at the hammock which reached to the right and left as far as the eye could reach, that this was the place & we must leave our horses here. Col. Foster asked how far to the camp. Ans[wer], one mile – adding – it is very bad & muddy – half of Maj. Nelson's battn. being left with the horses we proceeded into the hammock, the prisoner leading off, the rest following in single file. (By the by – Jim Boy & 15 indians went with us). Four soldiers followed the prisr., then the interpreter – next (after Col. Foster, Lt. Myers and myself) Jim Boy & indians – then Capt. Allen's compy. followed by the vols. We probably marched 2 1/2 miles into this indescribable swamp & crossed 14 creeks. We then came to a deep lake of brackish (or limestone) water; the point at which we arrived appeared to be a landing place – there had been a fire round which indians had slept perhaps a month before. Here our poor guide who was very miserable, confessed that he was lost but that he could find the place – he'd been used to going in & out of his camp by canoe. However, he did not seem to desire to go much further for he was certainly in too great a state of exhaustion to continue longer on the arduous service of finding a trail, by moonlight, when it is [a] matter of astonishment that he could precieve any resemblance to one. He had been three hours in the swamp & concluded to return before the moon became lost. So we faced about and were conducted back on our own trail by Jim Boy himself. When we went in I left my cloak under a bush previous to crossing the first stream. One company of foot was ordered to halt at the second stream where it waited till we came back. We came back to camp like folks coming home from an evening meeting when I learnt with conceivable gratefication that my tent had been on fire & was pulled down & destroyed. I put myself to bed by a large fire after changing all my wet clothes and when I waked up at 6 A.M. I found it raining hard & my bed full of water.

18th. Got another tent. Feel very much worn out. A party of the horsemen went out in the afternoon towards the swamp we entered last night. About half a mile from it they overtook two indians one on a pony the other driving a pack pony loaded with jerked beef. They made for the swamp but were overtaken. They would not surrender. One of them struggled desperately – he resisted the bayonet by seizing it & pulling the horseman to the ground who knocked him in the head with the butt of his gun – he whooped with his last breath. The bodies of both were brought to camp & buried. The youngest was too handsome to be called a man and every soldier called him the boy. He was six feet high & elegantly formed – his name was "Ista Jago" – the other "Woz Wackay". These names were told by Tsa wa no gay, our prisoner, who says they are Tallassy's.

19th. Major Wilson with some horse & foot was ordered out on the North side of the same swamp with orders to explore to the gulf. Maj. Nelson with horse on the south side while Col. Foster with myself (commanding Comp. H for the day), Capt. Lyon with his piece of ordnance & Jim Boy with 60 or 70 Creeks advanced on our trail of day before yesterday to the entrance of the swamp. There we left Capt. Lyon to whom was given half my compy. We then entered the swamp to the first stream & sent the Indians ahead to search for signs guided by Tsa–wa–no–gay, who before they left us was told that there were indians in the swamp – that he knew where they lay, that he had a whole day before him & must point them out or he would be shot at night. He seemed quite unconcerned. We waited an hour then felled a tree across the river, it was a large cypress & made a loud noise. We crossed this stream & went on to the next, constructed a sort of bridge by felling a tall tree on each side & uniting them by logs. Here a runner from Jim Boy informed us that the prisr. had chosen to follow the track he took on the 17th & a mile & a half beyond the landing where we turned back then, he had found signs made yesterday & would wait for us to come up. The Col. sent him word to go on till he found something real, that he would advance as far as the landing & wait there for him. Between 2 & 3 we had bridged our way to the landing. We made a fire & waited till sun set. We then took the daylight for picking our way to the mouth of the swamp where we left a guard over the horses & packs of the Creeks and proceeded with Capt Lyon to camp – where we arrived after dark. Jim Boy followed us in with 20 prisoners.

Sems.	Negroes
5 women (Amongst them	3 men
Tsananogay's wife & child	3 women
5 children	3 children
<u>1</u> girl	
11	

The grown negroes all talk English. Lt. Reeve went to Ft. Clinch at daylight with 4 waggons for forage.

20th. Rested from our labors. At 2 P.M. Lt R. returned with the forage.

21st. Very stormy all night. At day light the rain ceased. Marched at sunrise for Tampa. Course S.W. 16 ms. The Geor[gia] mounted men got 4 ponies – the creeks 12 from the Anuttilligay hammock. Passed the town of Eui–faw Tustenuggy[11] whose people are now mixed with the Tallassies (called Topkaligay) and another town where Black–dirt[12] lived. Encamped on a pond one mile from the latter. Talked with the prisoners about the war. Their conversation is very amusing. An intelligent one says that at C. Izard the indians were in earnest & that when they came on the second day the whites laid off from camp and then came in to surround them – and fired on them. She says the whites have cheated them so much they can not trust them and they so strongly believe that they were cheated at Camp Izard that they won't come to have any more talks. All the women & children were in the wahoo swamp throughout the Battles. They were to be left there & the indians (warriors) were to run thru' the pine barren supposing the whites could follow on the trail. At that place after the battle, Alligator's band was very selfish in getting plunder (which could not have been anything of consequence I think) and drove all the cattle, some of which belonged to other tribes, down towards Peas creek where they live – and on this account the other indians have fallen out with them. The chief of the Micasukies who was able always to keep the tribe embodied & active was killed at the surprise of Ft. Drane. The present chief's unable to do anything with them – they have scattered from him. Powel is a good warrior and a <u>gentlemanly indian</u> "the most gentlemanly indian in the nation – he don't take white folk's things – he never has even got a horse" – he would be a good chief if he had men – but alas! the Redsticks[13] are but <u>8</u>.

22nd. Marched a little before 7. Struck Gen. Clinch's trail at little before 10 – encamped on a run [creek] 18 ms from Tampa – having marched 18 miles today.

23rd. Marched 18 miles.

24th. Marched 3 miles to Tampa & encamped on the west side of the Hillsborough – camp Foster[14]

25–26–27th. Encamped at C. Foster.

28th. Signed receipts to Lt. Myers for the property of compy (1) on the promise from him that he will make good any difference I find in the quantity on hand when it can be examined and the quantity on his invoices. Drew pay for Dec. & Jany. from Capt. Sanders 129.00 – paid Reeve my mess bill 35$ (32.80 today).

Marched for Camp Lyon 8 miles [north] on the Clinch trail – rain all day – disagreeable. Capt. Allen with Comp. K goes round by water to meet us on the We–wa–ky i–ikak or Crystal river. Private Parsons of Compy. I missed in the afternoon.

29th. Rained all last night. Marched ten miles during heavy rain – encamped before noon. Some of Maj. Nelson's men discharged their loads instead of drawing them – he put them to climbing trees for punishment.

30th. Marched fourteen miles. Encamped at the point where the trail from Camp Lyon enters Clynch's.

31st. Marched six or seven miles and encamped in the morning in

an indian town at the southeastern extremity of the Anuttelligay. Maj.
Nelson was sent along the south side to reconnoitre the hammock. At
night he returned bringing a pony all saddled from which the indian
had fled. I suppose he was looking for cattle.

31st. of Jany 1837 (Continued) The Indian rode between two felled

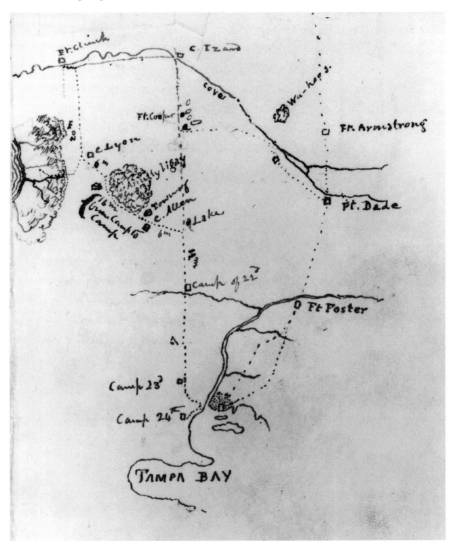

20. **Roads, forts, and camps between Tampa Bay & the Withlacoochee River**

trees whose tops intertangled – his pony could not get through and he
left him – committing his safety to his own legs.

February

1st. Burnt the town & left. Encamped 2 miles south of camp Lyon at Camp Chastilion. Rode to camp Lyon with 6 men & requested Maj. Nelson to come back to C. Castite.[15] At 8 P.M. everything being favorable in the highest degree – 3 rockets were discharged as signals to Capt. Allen on board the Stm. Boat. – No reply observed.

2nd. Sun one hour high left for the Swamp by our old trail. We had 3 comps., Alvord's, Tibbatt's & mine. The Col. had also his pioneers. We took dinner at the landing, 2 1/2 miles in. After which Alvord & Tibbatts with their companies were sent ahead to burn the indian town where the prisoners were taken. We took one of Lane's india rubber boats into the swamp, placed it into the first stream according to my map, with 7 men during dinner. She arrived at the Landing – having had a pleasant & easy trip & proving my map to be correct. After dinner proceeded to cross two rivers (branches) and encamped for the night. It was dark a short time when Mr. Alvord returned having executed his mission without meeting with anything of interest. A rocket was discharged – God knows what for! Very uncomfortable all night – cold – damp & noisy and no fresh water. Waggons to Ft. Clinch at daylight.

3rd. Early in the morning marched to Camp Chastilion. Lt. Reeve with the waggons arrived from Ft. Clinch at three o'clock whence he marched at 1/2 past 6. We laid at rest all day with the exception of Maj. Nelson's horse battn. They advanced to camp Wilson (6 ms) & encamped.

4th. Morning. Marched to camp Wilson & joined Maj. N[elson]. Encamped – Rain began soon after [and] held up at midnight. Two rockets were fired in the evening. It was so rainy that we could hardly see them ourselves. At 300 yds. they must have been totally obscured!

5th. Orders for the command to rest here today – Maj. Wilson with two companies enters the swamp to explore the Homosassa river. He requsted me to go with him in staff as Engineer. I have consented. We start at 10 o'clock – A.M.

We entered the hammock 3/4 mile from camp and in 400 paces came to a spring full of fish. 200 yds. further on we came to a broad deep rapid river leaping from the ground at our spring. The water appeared of a bright blue but was perfectly transparent. Some of the fish in it were two feet long. The major by my advice sent for the boat

& ordered me to descend the river in it. From 60 yds. it soon widened to 150 and varied in depth from 5 to 8 feet where I could see bottom. I went down more than a mile before I thought of waiting for the shore party. While listening for them we thought we heard the click of a lock & a footstep – but convinced ourselves that they were some of the wild sounds of a solitary place doubled by its echo. There sat a pelican over my head on the branch of a dead cypress looking like a tailor's goose.[16] At length I heard a gun but so slightly that no one else heard it. I thought it a signal for the boat to return. A moment after I had pushed into the stream for this purpose I espied Lt. Hooper[17] & small scouting party through a bend of the river. I joined him & we proceeded a mile farther when we met again up a very wide branch which I knew he would not cross. We returned from this point. Joined Maj. W. at the head of the river & all proceeded to camp.

6th. Marched at sunrise – though it was given out last evening that we should not move till one hour after. We arrived at Ft. Clinch at 1 o'clock & encamped at camp Nelson. No news from the steamboat.

There is a steamboat here loading with provisions for Charles' ferry on the Suwannee on Gov. Call's requisition who writes that the Indians have followed him homeward and are killing & burning between Tallahassee & St. Marks! What a fine commentary on his report of the "three victories".

7th. No news from the steamboat.

After breakfast this morning – the squaw Sally finely dressed & on horseback (accompanied by Tsa wa no gay) was set at liberty by Col. Foster who expects that they will negotiate for him.

8th. An Express from Col. Foster left camp early for Ft. Dade. I felt angry at its not being made known to the officers of the Regiment – and wrote the following note to Col. Foster.

Camp Nelson   Feb 8 1837

Sir,

I have the honor herewith to resign my appointment as Engineer to your command.

Very Respectfully
H Prince
2nd Lt 4th Inf

Lt Col Foster
Comg

Major Nelson with two companies of horse & two of 4th Inf. (Alvord & myself) is ordered to find the head of the We wa Kyiika & to proceed down it to meet Capt. Allen who with his company in Lt. Johnson's steamboat is ordered to ascend from the mouth. Both parties start early in the morning.

9th. Proceeded to the Chrystal river – and found it to be a large inland sea – were not able to determine the outlet. The wind was so high that the cloth pontoon was unmanageable. Encamped on a branch arising from a large spring.

10th. Early took 3 men with me & paddled round 12 miles at least in this archpelago without being able to ascertain positively its outlet. I climed a tree 70 feet high and looked over the land westward 8 or 10 miles. We saw an abundance of redfish, sharks & porposes – curlieu & a great variety of water fowl, not at all shy – indeed they were as tame as buzzards in a town. Examined everything that looked like an indian sign – found no fresh trace of them. Returned to camp at half past eleven A.M. having been absent more than three hours.

The whole command immediately moved for Ft. Clinch. About half way met a compy. of horses from the latter place coming to tell us that <u>operations must cease</u>. Two expresses having been received from Gen. Jesup with information that Jumper, Alligator & Abram have surrendered to him and that they are to bring in their tribes on the 18th till which time hostilities are suspended. Encamped at camp Nelson.

After dark, Capt. Allen arrived who reports that 10 miles up the river he disembarked, followed a trail which led him into two large camps, the second of which the indians were leaving as he entered it. A running fight ensued till near night when he retired, the enemy being beyond his reach. A Sergeant of Capt. Allen's compy. was shot through the heart. The soldiers say that he has continually asserted that the indians would kill him before this war could end. He was the only individual touched by a ball on the side of the whites. Lt. Johnson (Navy) with [?] men assisted in the chase.

11th. Tsawasnogay & indian Sally ought to have returned last night. I understand they agreed to come back in four days. Obtained leave of absence today to visit the mouth of the Withlacoochee – went down in steamboat & returned in the evening – delightful trip – two steamboats lying off the mouth – visited both. Learned with regret on my return that Corpl. Wilson of my compy. & a private of comp. (H) are missing. They rode out at 9 A.M. without arms to graze two horses. We suppose them to have been killed by the indians.

12th. Three comps. searched for Wilson & Pratt without success – Col. Foster's troops moved from Camp Nelson to get out of the vicinity of the Fort. Encamped about five miles up the river near a pond. The compy. of horsemen sent to Fort Dade returned at dark.

Private Arnet confined for stealing 40$ from Lowenstein. Lucia reported him. Arnet was called up to be searched. Lowenstein described his money – two 20$ notes Louisiana money – Arnet said he had not the money – I ordered Lucia to search him. Arnet yielded with a kind of bravado & defied him to find it – 20$ notes Union Bank of Louisiana was found under the lining of his stock. I asked him where he got it. He replied of a volunteer. What volunteer? I don't know what volunteer. I tied him to a tree – kept him tied half the night to make him tell what he had done with the other 20$. He would not tell but I thought the reason was the presence of the guard, his companions. I let him lay by the fire till morning, I then took him down to my tent & told him that I did so to give him an opportunity to confess before Lt. Reeve & myself. He then <u>confessed</u> and I sent him back to the guard.

Before daylight I was obliged to arrest the Sergt. of the guard for neglect of duty.

13th. Col. Foster went to Fort Dade in company with the Georgians who are ordered there by Gen. Jesup, Lt. Scott as adjt. went also.

14th. Visited Ft. Clinch. Wrote a letter there to Olinda. The two men lost on the 11th. arrived at Ft. Clinch last night without their horses – they had been bewildered in the woods & met with several adventures. They were out 3 days & nearly 3 nights without anything to eat – on one occasion were followed by indians but succeeded in eluding them.

26th. It is now fourteen days since we were left at this camp "Truce" by the Georgians, the Colonel & Lt. Scott. They are 14 of the dullest days ever evolved from the whorlegig of time. Not a word of intelligence from any quarter to tell us how the armistice is going on. The garrison at Ft. Clinch are worse off than we are for their place is not so pleasant as our little camp & they are equally cut off from the world.

A volunteer of ours being in the woods this morning with two companions had his horse shot dead under him being near a hammock. I was sent with a small party to reconnoitre the place – the distance was about 4 miles from camp "Truce". The horse was shot through the heart. About 20 yds. from him was a large live oak at the foot of which I took my <u>dinner</u> on the 14th of Jany. Behind this tree were the tracks in which the indian stood when he fired. Did he fire at the horse or at the man? At the horse I think – he was more sure of hitting him & flustrating the man – by which means he escaped.

March

3rd. Stmboat from Chs. Ferry arr[ive]d at Ft. Clinch with a few rumours of an absurd character.

4th. We sent an Express to Ft. Dade to see what is going on.

6th. The Express returned from Fort Dade with news that <u>Peace</u> was decided upon on yesterday by the indian council held at Fort Dade – or near there. We are ordered to march to Fort Dade.

7th. Lt. Hooper is ordered to Fort Clinch to remain there in command of the soldiers of our Regt. Wrote to Adams.

8th. At daylight moved from Camp "Truce". Alvord & myself passed half an hour or more at the bank of the river opposite C. Izzard. Just one year ago yesterday at sunset the hostile indians fired several volies from the spot on which we stood. We recognized Foster's Cavalier[?] towering above every other part of the spacious breast–work. Encamped 8 miles from C. Izard.

9th. Marched to the Big We-thlock-coochee, encamped on a prairie.

10th. Marched up along the Big With. to a pond 4 miles from Ft. Dade – encamped at 2 o'clk P.M. In the course of the afternoon we were visited by Rosl Lee, Ters Lee, Dr. Hults, Lt Rose[18] and by Chambers[19] & Mackay.[20] Capt. Lyon gave me a quid of tobacco.

11th. Marched to Ft. Dade.

Micco nopa says to Gen J. "You have driven him into a very bad swamp and he would be very much obliged to you if you would let him stay there."

The wagon master killed at Ft. Brooke 26th. Jany. was killed by <u>John</u> one of the pris.s <u>released</u> there by Col. Lane. Col. Henderson

is called "Old P[iss] to W[ind]ward", Armistead[21]– "Beeswax",
Churchill – "Front de Boeuf"[22]

13th. Rode to Ft. Armstrong – company Lt. R. W. Lee – we bathed
in the little Withlacoochee – I swam in it. It is about 18 feet wide at the
surface of the water – banks low and steep, a few logs only are left in
their places of Dade's last encampment which is two miles north of the
river & near a small round pond –it is encircled by one of Gaines breastworks. Five miles further is the battleground – the graves are neatly
palisaded – Moniac[22] is buried there and his grave is marked in the
same manner as the rest

21. Battlefield and graves of Dade's command & grave of Lt. Moniac

Fort Armstrong is here in sight a third of a mile to the north &
west. I got no sleep for the musquitoes – the fleas would have been
sufficient.

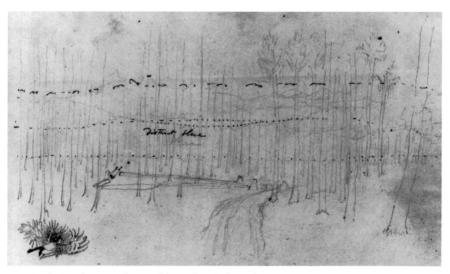

22. Dade Battleground [possibly a sketch for a future painting]

14th. Rode to the Wahoo Swamp – Compy. Lts. Mock[24] & Sing.[25] It is a vast place – secluded from the world – & a world of itself. A very heavy deep worn trail with many branches leads to it – for a mile previous to entering the swamp we were passing scattering indian dwellings. The first 1/2 mile (on the trail) was dry lofty hammock but from the declination of the ground I should think the right & left of the trail swampy – then a cultivated field say a mile in length, corn planted, stony – rocks piled up as on a yankee farm – excellent land – 1/2 a mile of a more dense & less spacious hammock – then a cluster of cypress trees growing out of a sheet of clear water about 30 feet wide and now 2 1/2 feet deep with hard sand bottom – both sides thick hammock, this is what Mock calls the "ne plus ultra"[. W] crossed on our horses and proceeded to the pine woods nearly 1/2 mile further. Beyond this point we went only 3/4 mile to a village – & then returned to Fort Armstrong to dinner having been about 5 hours. Am very tired & concluded to make another trial for a night's rest.

15th. In which trial I had no success. Got up early, took some coffee & left for Ft. Dade alone. Met Lt. Bainbridge[26] party half way between its forks – chaining off the road.

Cloud with two warriors did all the fighting at the Wahoo Swamp on the last day. Powel, Jumper – the whole force of the indians – happened to be in position farther to the right because <u>there</u> the whites were expected.

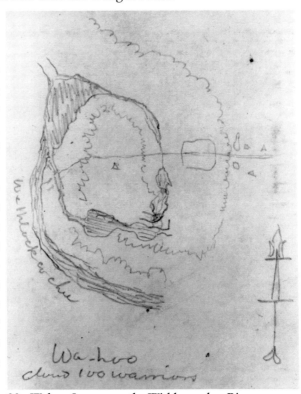

23. **Wahoo Swamp on the Withlacoochee River**

24. **Wahoo Swamp**

16th. Abra[ha]m came into camp & informed Gen. J. that Micco nopa had halted a mile or two from here.

17th. Miccanopa preceeded by Abram & followed by Alligator & others in procession passed the bridge & entered camp. He merely called to pay & receive respects. He would have a busines talk tomorrow. He is not bad looking, he is well dresed, robust – not old, having jet black glossy hair but he is very corpulent & pock marked.

Abram rode from Ft. Armstrong with Lt. Ross. Passing over the fatal ground of Dade – "Ah!" said he – "here is where those poor fellows were killed!" (Here he heaved a deep sigh) "Poor fellows! I was not there but I heard a great noise!"

18th. Council held with Micanopa attended by Alligator & Abram.

Emathlockas Emathla[27] arrived & met with a general welcome, as the council was about half through. The articles of capitulation were read and agreed to. Micco nopa touched the pen & made a speech to show that he was in earnest. He had come to shake hands with the Gen. & to lay along side of him. He should fight no more. "I have heard your talk and you have now heard mine. He above sees into our hearts & best knows whether we are in earnest or not. It is my lot to be in the circumstances in which I am and I say nothing about it.["]

Micconopa desired an agent – hoped to get Capt. Page[28] 4th. Inf. or Maj. Graham 4th. Inf. The Gen. appointed Maj. Graham temporarily.

25th. 2nd. Arty. proceeded to Ft. Foster to garrison that work.

27th. Morris' battn. Creeks proceeded to Tampa to be discharged.

30th. Gen. & Staff proceed to Tampa also Marines.

April

6th. Wrote to Houghton.

17th. Recd. an order to make a reconnaissance of the Withlockcochee from Ft. Dade to Ft. Clinch – to make a drawing & memoir. Lt. Brent[29] goes with this compy. & 10 Indians & Lt. Bowman[30] with 20 mtd. Georgians – we have two 4 mule waggons.

18th. Left Ft. Dade at 8 A.M. proceeded West 1/2 hour (one mile & a half), 2 [miles] NNW 1/2 hour to grass pond & old army camp (say 2 ms), 3 [miles] NW half an hour passed the camp of old Cloud[31] when on his way from ar–fus–coo–chee or short point to the Wahoo swamp soon after the commencement of host[ilities]. 4 [miles] North one hour & a half to the River (the inds. emetic <u>hepo</u> very common), say 6 ms. 5 [miles] N.W. half an hour to Camp Sabre. Whole distance 12 miles, time 3 1/2 hours rate, 3 2/3 miles per hour 10 1/2 ms rate 3 m per hour. Half an hour SE from Camp Sabre enter a large bend NE, at its maximum point the river is 40 yds wide & deep – banks steep (5 or 6 ft). Hammock broad but dry, mingled with cypress – followed the bank down 1/2 mile & crossed on a log below a point at which the stream branches forming an Island 1/2 mile square – both streams unite then in a large lake one mile long at least when the stream contracts again into several small ones across which a trail is worn leading from the Wahoo Swamp. Cloud, his two sons & cousin crossed here on the day that Gen. Jesup scoured the Wahoo Swamp. They had been there to see Powel & being afraid to travel in the day they commenced their journey at evening – the moon had begun to shine – he was in the open piney woods & heard the ground rumble. He discovered the army like a cloud coming directly towards him (returning to Ft. Armstrong). They dismounted, led their horses one side and skulked. The army was 2 hours passing – & their horses followed in its rear. They crept up & got them all (having secured the last one near Fort Armstrong) & then came to this place. Cloud went to his camp above Ft. Dade sending one of his sons ahead & keeping the other with him. The cousin went to Annuttilligay. This trail is called o–in–ninnh–sulka (trail where the creeks scatter).

19th. Started at 1/2 past 5 A.M. NE – 5 minutes before 7. The Withlacoochee presents the appearance (through an opening) [of] a large navigable river being clear from bank to bank & half mile wide, it flows on of this uniform width for some distance, the growth of both sides is large cypress.

[In the following descriptions, Prince used designations such as "15' to 8" to indicate time, not distance; hence, a quarter of eight o'clock]
At 7 o'clock course North
7 1/4 o'clock [written under Map A] 7h 23m [written under Map B]

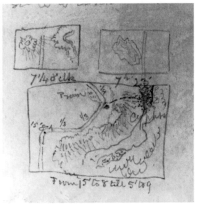

25. Map A   Map B   Map C

From 15' to 8 till 5' till 9 [written under Map C]

(7h 23' the river away off to the right out of view)

15' to 8 course E

10' " 8   "   NE (halt one hour)

5' " 9   "   NW (cross prairie)

5' after 9 "   W river hammock in sight bearing North pointing West distant one mile or more over prairie skirted by hammocks.

10' after 9, course NW, passing a hammock on our right – a trail strikes into the hammock due E – followed it to an old field cultivated 10 years ago probably – it goes round the south end of a large lake.

15' to 10 passed the hammock & lake.

5' to 10 passed tang[en]t to a lake extending 2 miles to the North – perfectly open on the side towards me at which is Pierces Camp.

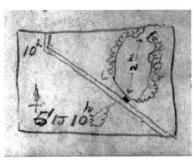

26. Map

10 o'clock struck the Tampa Bay Road course N.

22' past 10 h [o'clock] tangt. to a branch of the lake just mentioned to Cho-illy-hadjo's[32] (Crazy Dear's foot – "law-maker" or constable to the Tallassys) Town where Gen. Clinch encamped at the time Ft. Cooper was relieved by him.

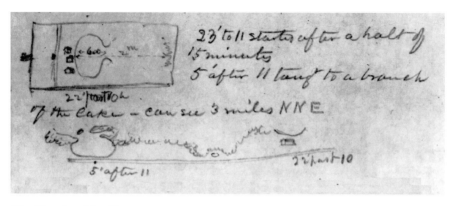

27. Map A   Map B

23' to 11 started after a halt of 15 minutes
22' past 10h [written under Map A]

5' after 11 tangt to a branch of the lake – can see 3 miles NNE.

5' after 11   22' past 10 [written under Map B]

10' after 12 arrived at Ft. Cooper having a lake on the right 500 yds. in diameter (the last 1/2 mile being NW)

10' after 12 [written under Map of Fort Cooper.]

28. Map of Fort Cooper

5h 40' time [elapsed]. Rate 3m pr hour, whole dist[ance] 17 m.

During the halt from 5' of 8 to 5' of 9 I went ENE to the river from the old camp – the distance was half a mile descending a hill through a thick hammock of very rich land – the river is skirted with very large cypress – the stream sluggish running North.

Evening went to Cho-illy-hadjo's town in search of two deserters from the 4th. Infy. Did not find them.

20th. Sent the waggons and foot [infantry] on to C. Izard & attempted to enter the Cove by the southern end. For this purpose left camp at 7 A.M. SE most of the way to Cho-illy-hadjo's Town – then S 15' past 8 – at Cho-illy-hadjo's Town, 35' past 8 at the forks of the Road, course SE 10' to 9 – the road borders a savanna – water in its center. 10 o'clock at the grass pond South of the Vernella Patch Camp[?] – turned & followed the course of the river – spent two hours riding round thro & over praries, hammocks & ponds – we were completely headed off & brought into the mil[itary] road – halted unsaddled & took shade – at the point of hammock where we were this morning at 5' past 9.

2 h & 20 P.M. started – 5' to 3 Scotts trail, 8 h 15' at Town, 4 h 20' at Ft. Cooper – halted 10' – 4h 30' left Ft. C[linch]. N.W.

at 6 1/4 h course N.[,] lake on right,

6 1/2 h   ”   N.W.   ”   ”   ”   5 ms & 600 yds Lane's camp

10' to 7   ”   N.W.   ”   ”   ”   (near) one mile wide in a NE line & extending 6 ms N. through openings. 5' to 7h Col. Foster's camp on this lake, course N. 7 h course N. Eneah Thlockeo Emathla's town on the opposite side of the lake (burnt by Rt. wing) bears E. 7 1/2 ['] lake & prairie extending 6 ms East near the road. 20' to 8. Extends 6 or 7 ms. S.E. 15' to 8, lake in which Scotts boat is sunk & commencement of the trail by which he entered the Cove. 9 o'clk P.M., arrived at camp.

General course from Ft. Cooper to C. Izard N.N.W. Whole distance from Ft. Cooper to C. Izard 16 miles, time 4 1/2 hours.

We tried to drive some cattle to day – they are as wild as dear – they run into the hammock & hide seeing you a mile off – "it will be as much trouble to catch them up as it was to catch up the indians".

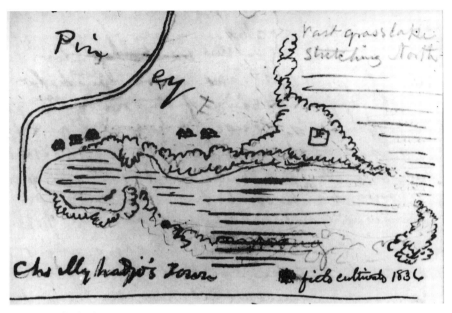

29. Cho-illy-hadjo's Town

21st. 8h 5' left Camp opposite C. Izard & followed a trail up the river, in search of an entrance to the Cove – general course (started at 8h. 5') of the river N.W. The trail followed its banks cutting off the bends & touching it occasionally – at 1/4 before nine touched the river near a small island & was obliged to deviate from it by a cypress stream – on emerging from the hammock crossed Gen. Clinch's battle ground of 31 Dec. The cypress creek faces an oak scrub ridge with very few pine trees on it. In this scrub were Clinch's men – in the cypress the Mikasukis.

At half past 9 passed through the breastwork in which Gen. Scott encamped on the night of 30th March & in ten minutes more entered the prairie from the North, on the southern side of which the battle of the 31st commenced. Endeavored to cross it but could not on horse. I followed the prairie round to the river where I could see the lake in the middle of the prairie united with the Withlacoochee – a row of cypress trees only marked where the banks of division would be if the lake were much lower – on the opposite side of the river the growth of cypress is dense & heavy. The stream is rapid of the usual width (say 50 y.) & the banks low but steep – the current here runs N.W.

At 12 o'clock started from the North side of the prairie for camp which we reached at 1/4 past two P.M.

Powell is telling Ansel, a negro, about this battle of the spotted lake, said that he was stunned by the wind of a cannon ball passing near him. He was carried off & did not recover for several days – the ball passed through the hollow cypress at which he had posted himself and "cut his breath" – "it went through the tree just as if it were fired close by!" He said too that he was very glad the Gen. did not come on further – he was glad to see him go back again – for he would have been obliged, had the troops advanced further, to "move his house" – but – "when he saw them go back from the creek to the pine ridge he went & staid at his old place".

Lt. Brent & myself crossed the river in a poncho together – went all over Camp Izard – visited the grave of him whose name the place bears & found it undisturbed – he sleeps quietly beneath a pretty overhanging oak.

22nd. At 7 A.M. started for Fort Clinch. Followed the river pretty nearly.

W 30 N till 7 3/4 o'clk A.M. then
W   "   " 8 1/4   "   "   "
NW "   " 9   "   "   "

left the River by going South a mile & a half to the road which I struck at Crane Island Lake, then WSW from 10 O'clock till 11 A.M. to Camp Truce, then W by N one hour & a half to Ft. Clinch. Country 7 ms. E of Ft. Clinch but spare & in open piney woods. A volunteer's horse gave out.

23rd. Remained at Fort Clinch – Brent sick. Hunted deer with Lt. Bell – started up three, Mr. B. hit one. Great many Deer. Kindly treated by the officers of Ft. C., Lt. Bell, Dr. Spotswood, Mr. Hoburn, Mid Morgan & Lt. Hooper. Watkins & Abadie[33] were absent, at St. Marks.

24th. Set off early with Ansel – accompanied by Lt. Bowman G.V. [Georgia Volunteers] & seven men – we are all mounted destined to explore the Cove. Lt. Bell & the Doctr. attended us as far as Crane Island which we found white with birds as usual. I left them constructing a raft on which to pass over to the island. They were working hard – jackets off, cutting down trees with hatchets & dragging them to the lake.

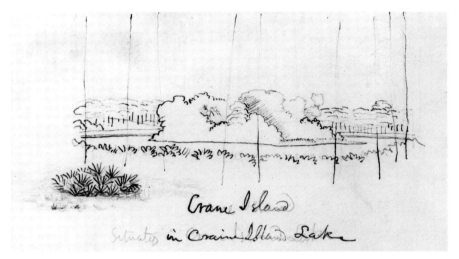

Crane Island

Situated in Crane Island Lake

30. Crane Island

Rested during the heat of the day on the river opposite C. Izard – and moved on again 13 minutes after three P.M. We occupied <u>nearly</u> an hour crossing the slough at the entrance of the Cove – all crossed in safety – three of us only stuck onto our saddles – it was not deep enough for the horses to swim & too soft for them to stand. The worst part was about 20 yds. wide. Passed through a large hammock (East) & camped in scrub & pine. It rained hard all night. I rolled myself up in my cloak wet and laid down on the ground with a blanket under me & went to sleep. I slept profoundly & was as comfortable as a mud turtle – my camlet[34] cloak was a good shell. I occasionally heard a clap of thunder which happened to be louder than the rest and once thought myself on fire – but these were momentary interruptions to my slumber.

25th. I was waked at 5 o'clock in the morning refreshed & bright as a lark. We set off immediately without feeding our horses in search of an indian town to make a fire of – for we had encamped in a region where there are no light–wood knots. In about an hour we found one, situated in a fine field in approaching which we passed through three very large hammocks & several minor ones.

In one of which there were streams running toward the Withlacoochee. Between the hammocks our path was through live oak scrub. The town was the best kind that could be for our purpose, the houses being built of indian boards & perfectly seasoned. Here we made a stay of two hours, took our breakfast, horses were unsaddled & fed. I rambled about the field eating blackberries & looking at the horses. The ground was covered with ripe blackberries an inch in diameter. Amongst the houses there was one in which powder & lead had been buried. There was the powder keg – the green hide it was done up in – the bullet–box & the hole in the ground lined with bark. The scene that took place here is easily filled up. The indians were all standing round this house – a vast crowded circle – the powder and & ball was issued to every one in equal shares – the old hide keg & box were thrown down at random & they all rushed off to a fight.

We left the field on the opposite side from which we entered and I think it was a mile through the hammock (which was full of palmetto sheds) to the open scrub. It commenced raining as soon as we started & I could not therefore make notes – a drop of water got inside of my compass at one time which perplexed me for the needle would stick fast by it to the glass. Our course was between SE and SSE. We next passed through a long series of oak scrub ridges separated from each other by furrows full of water, sometimes almost deep enoough for the horses to swim and 200 yds. across. Occasionally our trail was on a hammock island. At length we arrived at Powel's town.[35] Here Ansel was acquainted. He pointed out the field, the square, gave situation of the river and everything. All of which I found to be correct on examination. Powels' Town is on a little oak scrub elevation in a very large opening. There are no trees in sight except those on the hammock islands and on the river – no pine. The cattle pens are built of hard wood. Facing west you see nothing but hammock islands & scrub from the south round to north. Facing east the river runs from right to left. I followed a path NE half a mile to the river – the banks were overflowed to the depth of 4 or five feet. On the opposite side a blazed cypress tree was pointed out to me which marks the landing place for entering the Boggy Island. The usual way of approaching it is to come up in a canoe along the <u>creeks</u> – which are here so shallow that they are obliged to pick their way – and land at this cypress, cross a very muddy island on which this tree stands and then enter the Boggy Island. On the east side of the Withlacoochee a horse can follow the trail but not on the side toward Powel's Town. This island is accessible only by its northern extremity. It is a hiding place but little known even amongst the Indians. There is a field in the interior – here is where the negroes mostly concealed themselves in time of war.

It was now afternoon – between <u>12</u> and <u>one</u>. Our provisions were wet & spoiled and it was desirable to get to the camp of the rest of our party. By agreement this for tonight was to be at Fort Cooper about 6 or 7 miles to the west of us on the opposite edge of the marsh we were then in. To go out round this marsh the way we came in would be 30 ms to Ft. Cooper. So we concluded to try our luck for getting out by following the trail we travelled on all day & taking every branch of it that favored our course. We took the first trail to the right and went from island to island – often at a loss but appealing to the compass – sometimes crossing onto one island as a means merely of getting onto another though we went backwards to do so – sometimes going North to get onto a par-

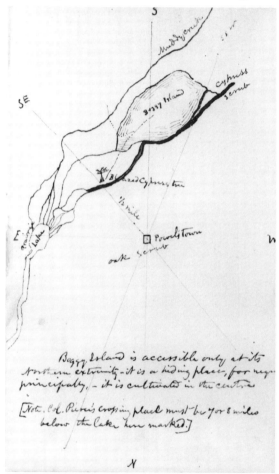

31. Powel's Town

ticular island that favored our course – sometimes south – our rate was about 3 steps for[war]d & one back. We at length came to a slough similar to the one we crossed yesterday – but wider & deeper & having some large rocks in the bottom with soft sand between them. <u>We all got across!</u> Everyone who attempted to ride across it was thrown but myself. We then after crossing a small island waded a slough 200 or 300 yds. wide nearly deep enough for the horses to swim – this wasted our horses completely. Not long after this we saw piney woods – these we reached (I believe by passing through a large hammock in which we lost the trail and had to go back & take it up again). We bounded on highly delighted for it was near sunset at reaching the piney wood & at last the top of the ridge [and] came to a large town of board houses. [O]n the other side of it our spirits were cooled down after descending the ridge a little way – by the sight of a perfectly black creek say 30 feet wide with an indian footbridge across it[. O]ur spirits descended below zero but immediately rose above par when by treading cautiously one fellow found it fordable. There was no hammock, we ascended at once amidst pines & blackjacks & found on the summit the other half of the town we had just passed. We rode round this & took the largest trail. To our surprise in less than half a mile it entered a hammock but we _____ halted. When to our chagrin, at the shore of a wide grass lake we saw the trail went straight across it! The grass was beat down in one or two furrows towards a piney point 1/4 of a mile distant and on the shore where we stood lay sufficient evidence of its depth viz. 20 or 30 green hides that had been used for boats. It was now some time after sunset. I proposed going back to the piney ridge & following it as far as it reached & there encamp if we did not get clear of this swamp. The Lieut. comdg. the 7 volunteers agreed to it. We passed on to a little hammock island at dark merely to see what was on the other side of it. The hammock looked impenetrable. I sent Ansel in on his pony to see if he could pick his way along. He found that he could & I followed him to see – & make up my mind whether to go back & camp or no. I was near saying we are far enough to Ansel when he moved a bushy limb from his face & laughing cried out "Here is de bu–ful pine barren". The shouts of the negro & myself soon brought the rest to us & in half an hour we discovered ourselves passing through an old camp of Col. Pierce's a mile & a half from Cho-illy-hadjo's Town & 5 1/2 miles from Fort Cooper. Ah! how my horse winnowed when he saw the lights of camp glimmering through the trees! I found Mr. Volmer in camp with a letter informing me that Mr. Alvord has joined (E) Compy (on 24th) and relieves me in command. I go to my own (K). Brent quite sick – put on dry clothing & had a capital night's sleep.

26th. Proceeded as far as Camp Sab[re], found the trail across the Wahoo swamp whence the latter bears east. The river is double at the place, the smallest channel on the eastern side. Encamped at Camp Sabre near a crossing place called O-ya-ninny-sul-kah.

27th. Arrived at Fort Dade.

May

13th. Ordered to Tampa. Reported respecting my topographical expedition.

20th. Lt. Alvord arrived at Tampa from Ft. Dade. In the night turned the property of E Compy. over to him & went on board the R[evenue] Cutter Jefferson, Capt. Foster. Got on board through the kindness of Maj. Churchill who ordered out the Garrison Barge & crew. It was after one o'clock when I went up over the side – went to sleep.

21st. At sunrise Capt. Thomas, Lt. Chambers, Lt. Searle & Dr. Byrne[36] (who had slept on board the Steamboat to be at hand) came on board & we made sail – at 10 A.M. boarded the US Ship St. Louis, Capt. Crabb, for one hour – at night anchored in the mouth of Espirito Santo Bay under Egmont Key.[37]

22nd. Sunrise made sail for Havanna. Stood our course part of the day with a moderate wind. Away with the morning breeze out sight of land – out sight of <u>Florida</u>!

24th. Made tolerable good progress with the night airs calm, pre-vailing all day–time.

25th. Tortugas Islands in sight 7 miles off – saw a prodigious turtle swimming – calm.

26th. Morning breezy – spoke ship Hermitage of Portland from N. Orleans for Liverpool – calm – breeze – made the maidens paps – dead calm.

27th. Morning, good breeze – <u>drifted</u> all last night with the gulf stream. Made the Pan of Matanzas before breakfast. Hoisted the en-sign for a Spanish coaster about 5 miles south of us going east before the wind – took no notice of it – fired a gun – she hove to directly. I never saw anything done so quick. In an hour we ran along side of her – ascertained where he was from, what he had & where he was going – ran in close to the shore of Cuba & steered to the westward wind free – how agreeable! The weather so pleasant, the wind so fine – so near the land – <u>high</u> glorious masculine land – it looks cool at the top of those hills – how different from a sand reef! Cocoa nuts & palms – cultivated fields, houses & hills we are passing at a gallop. <u>ecce signum.</u>[38]

32. Coast of Cuba 1

try again

33. Coast of Cuba 2

Here is a little river – a little town & a little fort – back are seen the Iron Hills – now for another:

34. Coast of Cuba 3

A hamlet, houses in a row & all alike (brown) – granite tower for a gun – at the same time that I am taking this the Moro [Castle] is in sight a long way ahead and seen over the land thus

35. Coast of Cuba 4

Here we are abreast of that Monastick [sic] looking fortification. See the Moro ahead there? Now we are off Havana looking into the harbor.

36. Havana, Cuba

A cloud with its belly full of wind & water swallowed us up as we were approaching the entrance to the harbor of Havana, we were obliged to steer off the land – out into the gulf again – at 9 P.M. perfectly calm – we are drifting <u>from</u> Havana – High ho! I'll go to sleep.

28th. At daylight we found ourselves near the villa & fort (1st picture) 15 miles from Havana, a breeze! Before the gale she bounds.

At 12 M.[noon] went in by the Moro & anchored off the city – odd! strange! curious! pretty! Took dinner on shore – Mdme. Martin's cornucopia & Mercaderes – Mr. Tacon[39] brought us tickets to the Ball this evening.

29th. The ball last night was on a grand scale, cost 2,000$ to get ready for it. It was magnificent. Girls all fat – few pretty – dance like a treadmill, get agoing can't stop. Dr. Byrne & myself undertook to walk home. Had a devil of a time . . . lay abed late this morning. Dr. & myself had a private breakfast which cost us three bits each. Longa – ponalis[?] lemonade & <u>ice</u>, ice creams, etc. Dinner in great style – evening passed – Governors garden.

30th. In the evening heard the <u>band</u> play in the Governors square. It played very slow tunes, extremely solemn, sleepy & sentimental. Its standard was a large paper lantern in the shape of a crown. The emblem seemed to be that the crown was trying to extinguish all light. It would not apply to the government of Havanna at the present time, for Tacon is a great man, a Regenerator. It is remarkable that he is unpopular with all classes except the military. With the rich creoles (i.e. the uppermost class) because instead of leaving the government of the place to them as in the hands of feudal chiefs, he governs himself (contrary to the usage of former governors). With priests because he has sifted them & abolished some of their outre formes – such, for instance as making everyone fall on his knees to their rag–baby when they promenade with it. With the law because they are obliged to conform to law – he has abolished gambling – taken the points off their stillettos – & the magistrates of different quarters of the city are responsible for the knavery committed in their departments – they must produce the thief in _____ days or go to gaol. This prevents the criminal & magistrate going shares as formerly.

31st. There are a great many poor men here in chains & at hard labor who were taken prisoners in Spain, fighting for Don Carlos for mere difference of opinion. They are banished to pick stone under a torrid sun.

June
1st. Went out to the Lero [Sero?]. Dined with Mr. Crugher, Chief Eng. of the Rail Road & Mr. Washington Hood. Visited Bishops gardens – called at Mr. Triste's. Mrs. T. passed us a cup of tea.

2nd. Escorted Lt. Chambers, Capt. Thorn and Lt. Searle & Dr. Byrne to the dock whence they went on board the Rev. Cutter Jefferson – found a smack bound to Key West – starts in the morning. Obtained a passport for which I paid 4 1/2$. Felt melancholy at the loss of all my own tongued companions & to console myself rode to the <u>punta</u>[40] – saw the grave yard – several heaps of human bones each as large as a meeting house.

3rd. Early got my trunk into a boat & went off on board the sloop Splendid[. I]n an hour after she started with a strong breeze. A [P]ortland brig left at the same time. I had seen the Capt. before but did not recollect his name.

6th. Morning – after a tedious passage of head winds & calms, arrived this day at 12 M at Key West. Taken on shore by Capt. Patterson, customhouse offr. Dined with Ollivella. Phew! <u>what a quantity of musquitos!</u> Took lodging at the "Quarters" board with Capt. Patterson who lives in the house over the water. I am commanding officer here to be sure but think I'd

> "Better <u>dwell in the midst</u> of <u>alarm</u>
> Than <u>reign</u> in this horrible place."

July

1st. Reced. orders to commence issuing rations to citizens &c. Took upon me the said duties – glad to have something to do.

[I am] Dwindled down to nothing – sick – billious attack – Judge Webb, Dr. Percival very kind.

Accepted an invitation to go to <u>Nassau</u> in the Sch. Caroline. A trip from this place must be beneficial to me. Mr. Olivella & Mr. Elsaurdi are going.

16th. (Sunday) Left K.W. for Nassau – <u>no wind</u> to day. Asa Tift left today for the North. Mr. Weaver[41] & wife left in the Cutter for Havana.

17th. Plenty of wind all night & dead ahead. We are crossing the Gulf – <u>nothing</u> in sight but a porpoise now & then.

18th. (Tuesday) at 9 P.M. on the Bank – water white – or light green – very shoal – see bottom perfectly plain (2 1/2 & 3 fath.) – <u>even ahead</u> in which case the first impression of an observer is that the vessel will ground. Here is the place for coral fans & sponges – no fish. Smooth pretty sailing.

19th. Wednesday noon – passed off the bank into the Gulf of Providence through the north west passage – here blackwater & heavy sea again, strong breeze (ahead), vessel beats well – appetite good. Sardines & bread relish well especially with an onion & good bottle of claret wine. Midnight squally – nearly capsized, water poured in over leeward side – dropped the foresail – righted. Contest between two thunder clouds! Magnificent, <u>Ossian–ic</u>[42] – sublime. Now one growls – now the other – now a flash athwart the dark features of one immediately returned by the other – the din increases as they bear down towards us until it is one continued scintillation & explosion. Each sound retorting with its great voice upon the other & brandishing shafts of fire. At each stroke the hurricane of their breath – and the existence–giving fluid – the blood of those superhuman champions flows with furious profusion – till quiet & <u>pale</u> they lie basking in the horizon beneath a glorious moon – mingled into one!

21st. (Friday) Morning. Providence Island in sight over the starboard bow. At 2 P.M. went on shore at Nassau, put up at Mrs. Fishers – took dinner ashore. Nassau is a very pretty town on the declivity of a steep hill. Set on three parallel streets which are mostly cut out of solid rock – it stretches along the shore about 2 miles –

37. **Statue of Columbus**

Fine statue of Columbus. The houses are mostly of stone. After dinner walked to the square on which the troops parade – it was sprinkled with red jackets.

Mr. McIntosh & Lt. Tew are boarders at Mrs. Fishers – they are from Turks Isle.

Sunday 23rd. Review of 2nd. W. I.[West Indies] Regt. – all black, drill well – officers extravagantly <u>militaire</u> – strutting, i.e. – sticking their bellies out.

26th. Visited billiard room. Dr. Stetson called – introduced us to his father in law, Am. Consul. Mr. Huyler.

27th. Introduced to Lt. Nichols, a large built & tolerably well made young man.

28th. (Nassau) 1837. Gave notice in the morning that we should sail at 11 A.M. Lt. Chuo told ____ that he regretted he did not know before that I was an officer of the Regular Army – wished to know if I really was – said he had travelled in America & received great attentions. Heard of a Ball – went to see it – went on board at 12 P.M.

29th. At 2 A.M. left with fine strong breeze – dead aft. At 9 A.M. having crossed the Gulf of Providence arrived at the North West Passage onto the G. Bahama Bank. Before dark passed off the Bank into the Gulf of Florida – having had a beautiful & entertaining day.

30th. At 7 A.M. off Indian Key. Hove to. Squall calm. A breeze blowing against us – beat "ready about", a hard line &c. At night wind rises.

31st. Early in the morning anchored in Key West – much improved in health.

In the case of my visit to this beautiful, though not very florishing town [Nassau] I paid a visit to the S[uprem]e Court then in session. There I beheld 8 negroes & 4 white men empannelled and a very prim, nay dandified looking lawyer addresing them as "<u>gentlemen</u> of the Jury". The almost weeping gravity of this declamatory champion seemed actually called for by the deep gloom that overhung his auditors.

> "In great King Alford's reign,
> Three mighty men were turned out doors
> Because they could not sing".

But could the ghost of that lauded monarch have arisen and viewed in his own land the prositution of his grand machinery of the Law it would have confessed that they might have been turned out in these days for lighter criminalities than a mere inability to sing. The indians may be right in saying that the negroes have the best sense. The redman the next in quality and the pale–face none – or very bad sense and no where will the question have a fairer trial then in this town of Nassau, where as fast as they serve their apprenticeship out they become free & entitled to all the privileges of the whites. The negro & the caucasian come in contact on equal ground. Cases might be cited where the former has had rather the advantage by the local government leaning to him though in the wrong – yet from the purest motives.

Here the politician must court the favor of his colored friends and flatter those whom he once commanded with an iron blow – his speech too in the House of Assembly – his maiden effort perhaps may be directed & retorted by the taunting lips of his former <u>Boots</u>.[43] It is almost needless to say that this is felt by both parties. And almost daily some trifles light as air increase the jealousy between them which displays itself more in marketing than otherwise at this time. The negroes buying everything saying they wish to live as well as the whites. I will say this for them, that they were very civil to me on every occasion & in every place. Those who were impudent in the street, that I saw, were so only to the groups of soldiers sauntering about – & it was probably because the latter seemed to make more pretentious strutting with his switch than were due to his black skin, mottled appearnace, white pantaloons & red jacket – considering that he was not so <u>very free</u>, with them, after all.

I saw an astonishing tree here which a bystander called a cotton wood tree – he said it was "excellent for razor straps" – it was lofty & covered an area of more that 200 yards in circumference. What astonished me most was the singular manner in which the roots brace the immense tree against the hurricane.

August   )
September)   a tedious succession of sultry days & crops of
October   )   mochitoes.

November
1st. Weather temperate – endurable – moschittos on the wane.
18th. Continues pleasant – quite agreeable – health improves – steamboat New Castle arrived having Maj. Mapes[44] on board.
22nd. Having been on board the Steamboat of Capt. Wilson (of Belfast) all the time since she arrived I went out over the bar in her

today as she departed for Tampa Bay. (Bourn DeCamp)[?]. I was sea sick.

28th. Saw in a N. York paper an order for a Ct. Martial to try Lt. Duncan. What can it be for!

December

3rd. Mr. N.W. Weston arrived, 9 days from N. York, with news from Eastport 5 weeks old.

5th. Dancing party at Messrs O'Harra's, Well's & Marvin's.

7th. Morning – left K. West for Tortugas – noon arrived at Marquis Keys, pretty harbor. Afternoon bird shooting – night weighed anchor & stood for Tortugas.

8th. Morning arrived at Tortugas Light House.

9th. Sailed on our return – at night were becalmed on the Quick Sands.

10th. Anchored in the harbor of Bocca Grande – very stormy – Moschitoes took possession of cabin, I stood in the storm all night.

11th. In time for dinner arrived in Key West.

20th. Dancing party at Mr. Weavers.

21st. Recd. orders to join my company via Tampa Bay – I am sorry to receive them but Major Hook[45] who procured them for me thought that in doing so he rendered me a favor. Key West is just getting agreeable. My health is getting good and I am expecting some clothes.

I am sorry to receive them but
Major Hook who procured them
for me thought that in doing
so he rendered me a favor —
"Key West is just getting agreable
my health is getting good and I
am expecting some clothes —

Jan 3.1838 · Left Key West in a
sloop for Tampa. *

6th A.M. — arrived at Ft Brooke

8th Assigned to the command of a
Detachment of 91 Recruits.

10th Marched with them for
Kissimmee

12th passed Fort of razer at
Pease Creek.

14th arrived at Ft. Gardiner & got
rid of my recruits found here the

* Joyful sounds may fill the brain
And mirth continue its hour of laughter.
But cooler moment come again.

38. Opening page of the Diary of Lt. Henry Prince for 1838

THE DIARY OF LT. HENRY PRINCE

1838

January

3rd. Left Key West in a sloop for Tampa.*

6th. A.M. arrived at Ft. Brooke.

8th. Assigned to the command of a Detachment of 91 Recruits.

10th. Marched with them for Kissimmee.

12th. Passed Fort Frazer[1] at Pease Creek.

14th. Arrived at Ft. Gardiner[2] & got rid of my recruits, found here

---

* "Joyful sounds may fill the brain
And mirth consumes the hour of laughter
But cooler moments come again
And sader thoughts do follow after.
Fay is the dance & music's power
Draws sweetly on the heart it fell
And life is uppermost in that hour
But Ah! we all must say Farewell.

Mid the broad rough ocean lies
Green as the first soft bed of Adam
A little spot where sunny skies
Are rivalled by the eyes that glad 'em.
Farewell to thee thou storm girt isle
Thou half intruder from the sea
May mirth on thee forever smile
Bold Pioneer of Liberty."

the 1st. Inf. Col. Taylor Davenport,[3] Maj. Loomis,[4] Cap[tain]s Day,[5] Taylor,[6] Mackern, Gwynne.[7]

21st. Col. Taylor[8] left Fort Gardiner for Ft. Basinger[9] – I remain at Ft. Gardiner till Maj. Graham arrives from Tampa whither he has gone to escort Gomper[?] & his party.

22nd. Saw Paymaster Larned[10] just from Gen. Jesup's camp via Ft. Basinger.

23rd. At noon Maj. Graham with the mounted companies K & D, 4th. Inf. arrived. I joined him taking command of Com. K and we left for Ft. Basinger in the afternoon. Marched three miles & encamped by a small river which empties into Kissimmee lake.

24th. Marched 18 miles encamped in pineywoods – surrounded by hammock prairies – get our water from hole.

25th. 23 miles further encamped on the Istopoga [Istokpoga] river (an old parson says John [Young?] been with me 25 years & you ought to preach as well as I – I can't do that but I can draw an inference – Well what from this text are the jackasses snuffed up the east wind – Why says John. I don't know what influence, but they couldn't grow fat on it.

A fellow said his horse could draw anything. Can he draw an Inference? Yes, if it don't weigh over a ton.

27th. Ordered with 26 mounted men (6 being indians) to explore Fisheating creek. Of which nothing more is known that that it crosses the road proceeding from Ft. Basinger to Ft. Deynaud.[11] At 9 A.M. set out. Encamped in a small cabbage hammock say 24 miles from Ft. Basinger. Took all my horses inside the hammock. If the indians come they will have to charge the hammock for all around us is flat prairie.

28th. Crossed Fisheating creek & explored it perfectly to its entrance into the great Lake Okeechobee – encamped in an oak hammock on the stream.

29th. Marched to Fort Thompson on the Carlosa–hachee [Caloosahatchee] for subsistence.

30th. Returning left Carlosa–hachee early & marched as far as Fisheating creek where I met Lt. McCrabb[12] encamped with a large train of waggons. Encamped alongside of him.

31st. Explored the country north of Fisheating creek to the Okeechobbee.

February

1st. Explored [till noon?] & marched to Fort Basinger. (See sketch)

2nd. Crossed the Kissimmee in pursuit of Col. Taylor who marched from Ft. Basinger on the 28th., camped at Jesups Bridge.

39. Road from Fort Basinger to Fort Thompson

40. Road from Jessup's Bridge to Camp

There is a more particular account of the last few days on the back of the order – to go to Fisheating Creek.

3rd. Marched from Jesup's Bridge to a smoking camp where there was a paper stuck on a tree, directed to me for me to file to the left – so I filed to the <u>right</u> after having kept on a mile & a half wondering what it could mean:

> "Camp
>   half past 8 o'c A.M.
>   If Lt. Prince arrives he will file to the left
>   & follow Col. Taylor who has gone towards
>   the Okeechobbie in pursuit of hostile indians.
>   J M Hill[13]
>   a a a G"

Entered Col. Taylor's Camp at 4 o'clock.

4th. Having yesterday returned my men to their proper companies I am now in comd. of my own (K) mounted. Mr. Grandin[14] is absent to Gen J. camp. Maj. Riley[15] comds. all the mtd. force & Maj. Graham the mtd. regt.

Col. Taylor having his waggons parked here marched along the eastern border of Okeechobbee to the (Payokee) grass lake on Everglades proper & camped. We of the horse being in advance saw many fresh signs – & took 25 or 30 ponies. The indians in this neighborhood are considerably scattered & it is no use to look for them – we may be a week catching one.

5th. Returned to the camp of yesterday morning. My mare got started in a swamp & ran with all her might – my head & left leg struck a cabbage tree & knocked me off – without receiving any other injury (like the man who had his neck broke). Lt. Grandin arrived at 1 o'clock from Gen. Jesup's camp. Says they are all tired to death with doing nothing over there & would heartily join our column.

6th. All march for Fort Basinger. Arrived at Jesup's bridge.

7th. On the way I left the column and made a visit to the Battleground of 25th Dec.[16] First went to the camp where are the graves of the killed. Then crossed the saw–grass quagmire – then through the compact cypress swamp to the shore or beach of the great Lake which lay before me like the ocean in a calm. No land was in sight from left to right. The bodies of indians where mouldering here & there near the trees where [they] fell.

41. Shore of Lake Okeechobee

The above is a correct representation of it including the camp of the night succeeding the battle & the graves. At sunset I came up with my company which I found encamped at Ft. Bassinger.

8th. Lay still.

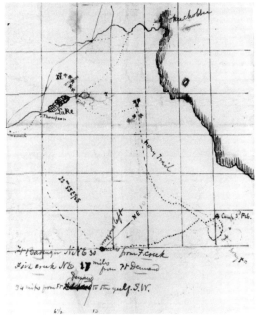

42. Area west of Lake Okeechobee

12th. Our mounted men (D & K) 4th. Inf. went up the East side of the Kissimmee a days march.

13th. Returned to Ft. Bassinger. Indian spies sent out by Col. Taylor. News of Jessup's truce.

15th. Express to Tampa.

16th. Maj. Riley's boat squadron left for Okeechobee to make a fort on the east side.

17th. News of Gen. Jessup's truce rec'd. <u>officially</u> – last night [from] Thompson. I got leave to go down to Fort Dennaud & see the people. Started in company with Chron Kerr[?] – and we slept in a waggon at Fish Creek.

18th. At Fort Dennaud to dinner. Dined on venison with Lieut. Plummer.

19th. In the afternoon Sergt. Totten with two men arrived with an order from Col. Taylor for me to determine the point on fish ck. where a post should be established. I shall start in the morning though I know that the only place for the fort is the site of Holate–chee's[17] camp. A steamboat arrived from the mouth of the river. Lt. Hammond[18] on board.

20th. Early started with Sgt. Totten & two men. Joined by Compy. at F. Creek at 12 o'clock. Eat some bean soup with them – took a fresh horse for myself & six men & went to Holate–chee's place where I met Col. Smith, Capt. Morris, Lt. Anderson,[19] Cross[20] & Bainbridge.[21] They had discovered that the best place for a depot was that [which] I mark[ed] out on the sketch of Fish–creek which I had given to Col. Smith. Col. S. ordered me to proceed next morning to Ft. Dennaud. I returned to my compy. & found that Lt. Hammond had taken possession of my tent to my infinite satisfaction.

21st. Marched to Ft. Dennaud.

23rd. Col. Smith informed me that he has recd. a letter from Col. Taylor & that the letter is expected here in a day or so.

25th. With my company I accompanied Col. Smith on a reconnoitering expedition for four days. The Col. finds provisions for himself & me & I find a tent for both to sleep in. Marched south about 20 miles & encamped – deer abundant.

26th. Followed a pony trail south west to a monstrous specimen of a full blooded cypress swamp. I went in on foot with one of my men about 1/2 mile but could imagine no end to it & returned. To make it perfect it required merely a few ball whistling thro' it [&] some of the leaves dropping. Took a NE direction & camped 4 or 5 miles S.W. of where Col. S. parked his waggons on his late expedition.

27th. Returned to Fort Deynaud.

28th. Sick

March
1st. ditto

2nd, 3rd, 4th, 5th, 6th, ditto.

7th. Better. Col. Smith with all his waggons & forces left this post for the cypress which I went into the other day. I rode out with him two or three miles & took leave. Compy. K to march tomorrow morn.

8th. Left Ft. Daynaud with my company for Fort Bassinger – crossed Fisheating Creek & camped 3 miles from it & one mile from the train of waggons which left Fort Deynaud day before yesterday.

9th. Two horses of mine & Lt. Hill's all missing. Sent men in every direction to find them. Detached a Corpl. & three men to F. eating Creek with orders to camp with the waggons tonight. Arrived at Fort Bassinger.

14th. Holate–chee came from Tampa says he saw plenty white people at N. Orleans. They can't [have] these in Florida. They are just like ants so thick that they are rolling over & over each other.

The remains of the officers killed at Okeechobbee on 25 Dec. brought to this place & deposited in the magazine. They are to be taken to Tampa whence Col. Thompson's[22] go to N. York & the others to Jefferson Barracks.

15th. Holate–chee left for Gen. Jessup's camp.

28th. A party of the indians arrived on the way to Tampa.

29th. 4th Regt. ordered to Alachua C[ount]y to rendesvous at Miccanopa to start early 31st.

31st. Moved off about daylight and camped at 12 M on a small streamlet of excellent water running out of a bay gall hammock into the Kissimmee – 8 miles from the crossing of Istoc–poga outlet. Buchanan with the party of indians who left Ft. B. yesterday evidently slept here last night.

April

1st. Encamped in pine woods near a grass pond that is almost dried up. The fires of Buchanan's party are still smoking here so that he must arrive at Fort Gardiner tonight. Major Graham arrived in the night.

2nd. Arrived at Fort Gardiner at 11 o'clock. Lt. Buchanan's party of Indians left about two hours ago. The place is much changed since I was here – it is beautiful. The Fort is completely shrouded in heavy foliage. The pickets are slightly seen between the trunks of the oaks as is the Kissimmee & its hioppo[?]. Maj. Graham left us at 12 to pursue his way to Tampa.

43. Fort Gardiner

At night Major Graham's brother arrived & Lt. Pew from Gen. Jesup's Head Quarters going to Tampa. They bring a letter relieving Col. Foster from this command & ordering him to Tampa to take command of that post & superintend the erection of barracks which proves that our regiment will be stationed there this summer. Gen J. it is said <u>talks</u> of a summer campaign! The flies & mosquitoes are so bad in this region <u>now</u> that my horses almost go mad. How bad may they be in the summer then?

3rd. Left Fort Gardiner and camped at Buffalo ford 16 miles from there & 12 from Ft. Frazer. Here again we meet the smoking embers of Lt. B. & the Istee–chattys.

4th. Passed Pease Creek and camped a mile this side – Buchannan left P. Creek at nine this morning with his indians. Rec'd. a letter from home via K. West.

5th. Camped on the Alafia. Found the ring I lost January in the sand. Received an Express in the night from Col. T. ordering Col. Foster and all the companies he commands to Tampa & to stay there.

6th. Camped at Ft. Brooke. Now Weston has failed very much. He was out though near his tent – but looks like death.

7th. Weston did not get up in the morning – said he was not so well. Carried Doctor Abadie to see him. The Dr. examined him very carefully & prescribed for him – told me that he could not live. Weston says someone stole 150$ from him.

8th. Called often to see Weston. Paid attention to everything he appeared to want – and offered him to ask for everything. He said he should want a hundred or a hundred and fifty dollars – which I said he could have without any trouble.

9th. Awoke early and called the first thing on Weston. He did not appear to me so well but said he felt better. I observed on his table a work on Christianity which I never saw there before. He breathed harder than usual. I asked him if he had not passed an uncomfortable night or was not under excitement. He said as comfortable as usual but had just been coughing. I said I would go & take my breakfast & return to see him. After an absence of 3/4 of an hour I was proceeding to his tent when Dr. Abadie told me of his death.

(Night sweat – held his hand – pulse quick)

News that the mail from Ft. Dade on the 3d was missing. I am ordered to be on the road to Miccannopa immediately with my comp. At 4 1/2 P.M. everything being previously arranged we buried poor Weston alongside of [?] who was buried the day before I arrived at Tampa this time. Order of procession:

Dr. Steneka accompanied by Lt. Babbit,[23] Lt. McKensie, Col. Davenport.

Corpse borne by 8 soldiers & pall bearers Lt. Casey, Lt. Stokes,[24] Dr. Abadie and myself with scarfs.

Officers and citizens. The Episcopal service was read at the grave by Dr. Steneka.

It is impossible to [– – – – – – – –] in this peculiar case [– – – – – – – – – – –] as do not leave [me exertion of deserting him. Poor fellow!] He died uncomforted! & with a broken heart!

10th. I was fairly worn out yesterday. I could not sleep all night – tho. very sleepy – & expect every moment to be ordered to proceed. The mail goes at noon and I cannot write by it to Mrs. Weston – Lt. Casey anticipates as much & says he will write.

11th. At daylight left Ft. Brooke. Camped 4 miles from Ft. Foster.

12th. Passed Ft. Foster at breakfast time, camped at Gaines' first pen 8 miles from Ft. Dade.

13th. Dined at Fort Dade and proceeded beyond the Little Withlocoochee [river]. Two miles from Ft. Dade passed by Gaines' second pen.

14th. Three miles from [north of] Little Withlacoochee passed Gaines' third pen which encloses Major Dade's last camp. Four miles farther Dade's Battleground. The road to this point inclines much Eastward (NE at least). Camped at the warm spring 11 miles from Dade's B.gnd. Here is Gaines' fourth pen. Captured a sorrel horse today.

15th. Met the mail carriers. These men well mounted and armed. Passed the grave of the mail carrier who was killed the other day. This is near Opilchopoochee[?] town. Camped 9 miles from Ft. King.

16th. At Fort King by breakfast time. Encamped 7 miles on the road to Miccanopa. A train of waggons going to Ft. King arrived & camped at the same place.

17th. Met a mail, two horsemen. They were on a clean gallop. Arrived at Miccanopa. They say the indians are plenty about here. They are shooting at all stragglers and mail carriers. Their object undoubtedly is to keep people from scattering so – to make the whites travel in force & then the indians can see them & watch them.

18th. Our orders are to clear the country between the head of Blackcreek & the Suwannee of indians. The major says we must move tomorrow morning. Force [on] foot 200 – Horse 54. He seems to expect to fight. The Spirit of Sam Jones[25] pervades these woods if perchance he is not here himself.

19th. Two horses stolen from the fort at midnight – a shower made the road perfectly smooth a little before – tracks now perfectly plain. They entered the hammock which reaches to Fort Drane a short distance off. With my company & a cracker for a guide I started round this hammock to see if they had left it. Four miles from Ft. Drane I found they had come out but finding it day [dry?] I suppose had entered it again. I sent the guide and 20 men dismounted into the hammock but in less than an hour they returned unable to follow the trail through the thick undergrowth. Retd. here to Micannopa. Maj. Riley leaves me here to rest till morning when I am to overtake him – he goes out 4 miles or so.

20th. Started at 1/2 hour before sunrise. The crackers said they made an agreement with the Major (Riley) to go round by McIntoshe's with my compy. & find him at his camp tonight – but my compy. not being ordered round and I not having heard a word of conversation upon the subject, conclude not to take the compy. round. However, I sent 20 men & the crackers & that will do just as well.

Overtook the Maj. at the Wacahoota. Here we all waited for the rest of my men & encamped. This is a prairie of a medium entent. 7 or 8 indians were killed here in [blank] by Col. Wanch. There is a bone here & a skull there & it was the sight of these that first led me to ask if there had not been a battle on the ground. The reply was no battle – 7 indians were killed here. The land is very good from Micinopa to this place.

21st. The men I detached yesterday found some very fresh tracks & all seemed to be making for the Ocklawaha where there is no doubt a collection. Captured 30 or more cattle – sent them to Miccanopa – our course is now to the Grand Prairie. The spot on which the Indians commenced the war. My ride nearly all day has been in the thickest kind of hammock, without a trail or path. My face is badly scratched to pieces. The signs were 4 days old – of mounted indians proceeding towards Ocklawaha. We emerged from the hammock onto Paine's Prairie & seeing our waggons about 2 miles off rode up to them & camped.

A heavy growth of timber snakes out into the prairie from the South side, called Black point. I suppose it is 3 miles from this camp. It was there the Indians opened the war by attacking some waggons in which there was much ammunition.

The train was guarded by about 40 volunteers who fled at the first volley. Col. Warren[26] with a battalion of Floridians at that moment came onto the prairie just here where we are camped. But was too late to save anything. The ammunition was taken, the waggons burnt. 4 vols. killed, 16 wounded, so says my Cicerone [guide] who was present with Warren. Ansel's horse wounded by a cow.

22nd. Rode in hammocks all day. No signs. Turkeys & deer. Camped 17 miles south of the Santaffee.[27] At night a company of Volunteers arrived near us and camped.

23rd. Marched to the Santaffee & crossed at the <u>Flat ford</u> where we camped. I took a corporal and six men from my company and rode twelve miles to Fort Harlee[28] where I passed the night with Lt. Brent. Here I met the mail from Tampa & the mail from Blkcreek. From the first I learn that Gen. Jesup has returned to Tampa from Fort Dade. The other brings newspapers containing the order for us to go to the Cherokee nation.

24th. I overtook the command of Maj. Riley at 10 A.M. on New River. We all encamped at an inhabited plantation where we got plenty of buttermilk. Sentinel fired (wild cat)! Shot dog.

25th. Crossed a creek – thru the Black creek road to Miccanopa – thru another creek & camped on Ockawilla Lake – up to this date the signs are all a fortnight old – & all arriving at the Ocklawaha. At present we are on a large trail of this description.

26th. Camped at the Waterpen. Visited the Etoniheh prairie today. Found no fresh sign.

27th. Encamped at Micannopa. (Maj. Riley would not let me water my horses.)

28th. Lay still at Micconopa. Commenced making my quarterly accounts for the last quarter. Commenced the Muster Roll also. Wrote a letter to Mrs. Weston. The express from Ft. King arrived – was fired upon near McIntosh's.

29th. One of the sentinels fired at an indian in the night[. H]e is supposed to have been mistaken. He says the indian fell & kicked & then jumped up & ran off. Ordered to get ready to march in search of those indians who fired on the express last night. Maj. Riley goes himself. The command consists of Capt. Tompkins,[29] 2nd. Dragoons & his company mounted, my compy. on horses – together with Lt. Hooper's & Lt. Hammond's companies on foot. The horsemen made a futile attempt to ride thru the Orange Lake Hammock. It was quite impossible. In McIntosh's old field we found the track of the indians & all three of the guides counted the Indians to be ten in number. We made a camp of the waggons & commenced following the track – found it tedious & difficult. We had once lost it, found it again & lost it once more; were halting for the guides to take it up again, when a party of horsemen rode up to us (from the fort): "The fort is attacked Major, two killed & three wounded" exclaimed the Sergeant commanding them. The Major ordered all the horsemen to dash forward to the

Fort & away we went. Fifteen or twenty men were swimming & fired upon[. T]wo of them killed and a third mortally wounded & the fourth is expected will survive his wound. Scoured the hammock round the pond. Saw where the indians distributed clothing – waggons & all came to the Fort this evening.

29th.

30th.

May.

9th. Wedneday. Arrived at Ft. Harlee with my company at break-fast time, having left Miconopa two hours by sun the previous evening. Found a volunteer in command – all the regular soldiers gone. Capt. Smith thinks from his instructions obtained from Gen. Eustis that he cannot obey Major Riley's order & will wait the decision of the former which he expects tomorrow, in reply of a communication made since my arrival.

10th. Supposing that I will be ordered to command here, I put my company in the barracks and informed Lt. Williams[30] that it would be well to commence turning over his property to me. He is engaged making the papers. Here is a fine place truly! Over–run with crackers who complain of drunken soldiers insulting their families and slyly selling them the liquor. Received the Commissariat & Ordnance stores from Mr. Williams and now I will go to bed. Mail from Tampa arvd. – was fired on in the Orange Lake Hammock again. Received the Sub-sistence and Ordnance stores from Lt. Williams. Smith gets no reply from Gen. Eustis.

11th. Friday. Examined all the Quarter Master property but shall not sign the papers till the question of Capt. Smith is settled. A little skirmish took place at the Nat[ura]l Bridge yesterday. This afternoon I found Martin my acting Commissary Sergeant <u>dead drunk</u> near the is-suing house. Took Donnely to perform the duties. Dr. Forry[31] returned.

12th. Lieut. Ross & his Company arvd. from Newnansville. Mail from B. creek arvd. No answer for Smith. Eustis has gone, Twiggs takes his place. Smith sends a special express to the latter to return tomorrow. (Mem[orandum]: witnesses in case of Martin – Corpl. Lynan, Thos. Johnston; they saw him in the issuing store with volun-teers this morning – the store broken open).

13th. Took a short ride. Lt. Wall[33] arvd. from Newnansville. Smith's answer from Twiggs is that he ought to have obeyed Maj. Riley's order. Smith now sends to, & waits for, Maj. R. to decide the question.

14th. Monday. An affray in the "town" today. The volunteer guard in taking a drunken citizen was fired on by the latter & the fire was returned. The Sergeant had his left arm shattered. I assisted the Doctor in amputating it. The drunken fellow was hit in the right hip near the joint. Mails from B. creek, Tampa & Newnansville after dark. Major Riley repeats his order to Smith to leave the post but lo! an order from Tampa, from Gen. Jesup directs him to relieve me & my compy. from this post & me to go to Miccanopa again. So I shall be off tomorrow. Farewell ye Crackers! & ye cracker girls & a farewell ye <u>one</u>–<u>roomed</u> log houses where lives, & sleeps, a generation. Farewell the dirty foot, slipshod, but never knew a stocking; the unwashed face; ropy hair; the swearing, lazy, idle, slut! Ye slouched hats & grandsires coats, goodbye. Ye drinking, drawling, boasting, cowardly sliggards – Fare ye well!

15th. Tuesday. Met Capt. Jock Munson at the Beu–tra[?] branch, Lt. Caldwell also & Lt. O'Neal[33] & Dr. Clark.[34] Camped at Micconopa.

16th. Lay dormant and **17th** too.

18th. Scouts round the S. side of Orange Lake beyond the cabbage hammock – found no signs – caught some young turkeys in the grass – returned to Micconopa.

19th. dormant.

20th. Scouts on the North east corner of the Alachua prairie – fresh signs – could not scour the hammock it was too large – rode thro[ugh] it as much as possible – returned to Micconopa meeting Gen. Jesup & staff between Fort Crane & the former place. Chambers not with him.

21st. dormant.

22nd. I tood (K) & (D) Companies both mounted & went out with three days provisions & forage. After looking about the Western side of the Alachua Prairie a little, I crossed over to "Fort Clark" a little settlement of about 20 men & their families, 7 or 8 miles N.W. of the prairie. As Newnansville was ascertained to be only 12 miles off I went on there & encamped beside Lt. Hooper's Company (G). This is the largest settlement in the interior of East Florida. There are 500 people here. There is a court house here & justices of the peace. It is a desirable station for Florida, butter, eggs, milk, etc. being plenty. The inhabitants however deserve no protection from regular troops for concealing the murderer of one of Lieut. Hooper's men. The man was mistaken for somebody else[. W]hile proceeding to the Garrison after dark he was followed & stabbed in the back. He ran – was chased – and stabbed over & over again – till he fell. A blow on his head with a hammer then closed his conciousness of existence forever, & he died on the spot.

23rd. I went to "the funnel" – where some brooks sink into the ground – a pond 129 feet in diameter with almost perpendicular high banks. Stepping onto a large loose rock, I frightened an old duck out from under it into the pond – I was going to shoot her but at the moment discovered her brood (little yellow things) swimming off to her, whistling twee – twee – twee – twee – ! and I altered my mind. The old one crossed the pond immediately where she was attacked by an Alligator. She flew to a side of the pond equally distant from the Alligator & ourselves & sat watching her little <u>whistles</u> while the Alligator ran to her with all his velocity, sank under her and was about to come up when she flew to the flock. The Alligator was there in a moment but as he was approaching the old creature betrayed the utmost agitation – now looking at her young & apparently saying something commiserating to them – now turning to the approaching <u>jaws of destruction</u> & almost flying into them herself – now she faces them – they arrange themselves around her thick breast of down – & there they are naturally billing & cooing! Now the Alligator sinks! A moment – and the old duck squawking flies up and the Alligators mouth, wide open, like a pair of scissors cames out of the water. He darts at her again – she is willing to run so long as he will follow her. When he turns towards the young, she turns. At length he gets to the brood first & getting one gosling in his mouth closes his jaws with a slam & disappears. The old duck now commences a retreat for the rest. She makes them swim as fast as they can. They found the first place they tried too steep. Here the Alligator took another young one. They tried another place of the bank & walked out of the water (A skunk or a fox I suppose ate them up that night!).

From this place I proceeded South westerly 6 or 7 miles to Kanopa-haw[35] thence to Wacahooty where I encamped.

24th. Returned to Micconopa before dinner. Orders are here to prepare to go to the Cherokee nation immediately.

25th. dormant. At night two comps. of Dragoons, Capt. Fowler[36] commanding arrived.

26th. Turned over company horses.

May		June
Tuesdays	15–22–29	5–12–19–26
W.......	16–23–30	6–13–20–27
T.......	17–24–31	7–14–21–28
F.......	18–25	1–8–15–22–29
S.......	19–26	2–9–16–23–30
S.......	20–27	3–10–17–24
M.......	21–28	4–11–18–25

27th. At sunrise left Micconopa for Black Ck. Encamped at Fort Harllee. The citizens sold a great deal of whiskey to our soldiers – several drunk. Being Officer of the day I stopped it completely. I captured in the course of the night about 5 gallons on its way into Camp! The night passed off without the slightest disturbance.

28th. Rode forward & took a nap at seven mile house while the troops were coming up. It begins to look more countryfied along the road – the farms are occupied all along to the Creek. Camped three miles from B. Creek near Roxana Tyner's.

29th. Morning at Blk creek. Lt. Hooper arrived with his company at night.

30th. Hooper & myself with A & K [companies] embarked in the Steamboat Wm. Gaston. Maj. Riley, Hammond & Bates[37] with G & D in the Charleston, our waggons are carried in the John Adams – our first destination is Savannah. In descending Black Creek I took notice of Herbert's Battleground. His men were completely concealed from the indians behind a steam mill & the bank of the creek. The steamboat was in a cove or small bayou & very near the mill so that Herbert's landing was perfectly covered. It is at the mouth of Black Creek, on the right bank. The perpendicular ridge extending from the mill to the left about 8 feet high, and with the mill furnished a completely sheltered place. He had 15 men.

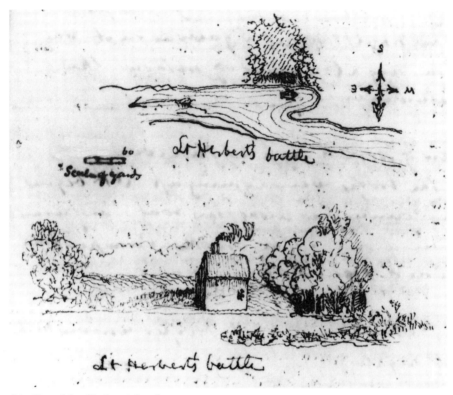

Lt Herberts battle

44. Site of Lt. Herbert's battle

It was nearly sunset when we reached the mouth of the St. Johns River. The tide being too low for us to cross the bar we remain here all night with a cabin <u>full</u> of musquitos. The smoke of the two boats ahead of us remained in sight after we anchored.

In coming down the river today we met two pretty steam boats going like the wind. We passed Jacksonville on the left bank of the river, a little town growing up under the auspices of the war. It is rather smaller than Key West Town.

Black Creek is broader & deeper than the Withlacoochee. The banks in some places are pretty high.

31st. At half past nine our boat is under way again pushing right out to the open ocean. I got drowsy & went to sleep in the heavy seas. Waked at one o'clock to see the last end of Florida. Vile Country! I have risked my life three years for you! As the worst – most unwelcome – occurrence that could happen to your heartless population, I wish that your Indian War may speedily terminate! And you left to work your bread out of the soils with neither Uncle Sam or the Indians in the way of your plundering hand!

Here is the town of Fernandina and then, beyond the St. Mary's river, are the tops of the houses of the town of St. Mary in Georgia. The first is on Amelia Island, where there are 15 young likely unmarried ladies & not a <u>single</u> gentleman. We are now in smooth water which reminds one of the Raritan, a crooked channel bordered with wide marsh grass. We begin to pass a series of low arable islands. Island succeeds island, nearly all have plantations on them, some of them exceedingly beautiful & having a light house as well as a plantation. Here is where the Sea Island cotton is raised. That raised immediately on the shore of the mainland is better than upland cotton but not equal to the Sea Island. An hour before sunset we entered St. Simons Sound and passed the town of Brunswick, not in sight however. At sunset we had passed Dr. I. Hamilton Cooper's vineyard, sugar plant etc. – a beautifully cultivated spot. Before dark we saw close to our channel the remains of the Old Town of Fredrika, the first town built by Oglethorp. A Fort is placed at the apex of a bend in the channel & commands both arms of it. The walls and chimnies of some of the old houses are standing & are made of Tavarino (a cement of shells). The two places last mentioned are on St. Simon's island which is long & has a great many fine cotton plantations on it. About half past nine P.M. entering the 3 mile cut – made by Gen. Oglethorp – our steamer grounded and it was 12 before she was again at her speed. The three mile cut creek joins the Alatamaha & Darien rivers.

June

1st. First day of summer! Going with all steam & speed. Character of our track the same as yesterday with the exception of our being obliged to stop & turn the boat with ropes at some "points d'[?]" in the narrow creek. In this way we have lost some time – but we go along gloriously – it is pleasant travelling!

Here is a pretty seat called Thunderbolt [Georgia], only 4 miles from Savannah by land – but we are 12 miles off by water. At one P.M. arrived at Savannah. The harbor bordered with level nice plantations brilliantly green, is very elegant. The city[,] almost as large as Portland[,] is neat & the quays are lined with vessels of the largest class. I begin to think we have entered the region of the United States again. Maj. Riley had everything ready for our reception onto an upriver boat, to which we transferred ourselves & put off up the Savannah river. For some miles up the environs of the city are highly cultivated. The banks are low – the river soon becomes narrow and lined with hammocks of live oaks. It is very crooked & the water muddy.

2nd. Still on board. Last night a drunken man fell over & passed under the wheel – nothing since has been heard of him. We have a strong current against us. Commenced raining at night. One man swept overboard by a tree rescued himself.

2nd. [Continuation] A pleasant day – an hour after dinner the cry of "man overboard" alarmed us. I saw him from the deck at the surface of the water. The exertions to save him were not prompt on the part of the men who saw him fall and the poor fellow drowned in our sight. The moment I saw him & saw no one putting off to save him I got into a half sinking canoe & paddled as fast as I could but was too late. This river water is so deep colored with red effluvia that nothing can be discerned below the surface. I never saw him after I got into the canoe.

3rd. Rainy all day.

4th. In the morning before breakfast we landed Lt. Hammond at Silver Bluff. Thirty miles (by water, 15 by land) from Augusta [Georgia]. It rained all night last. Arrived at Augusta in the afternoon.

5th. Marched through the city to the U.S. Arsenal 3 miles out.

6th.– 7th. Lay preparing for the march to N[ew] Echotta.

8th. At sunrise we moved from the walls of the Arsenal & marched 16 miles or more.

9th. Marched to Reesville [Ga.] (one dwelling house, carpenter shop, blacksmiths, bridge & mill).

10th. Encamped half a mile out of Washington [Ga.].

11th. Passed through Washington before sunrise & marched 18 miles to Buffalo creek.

12th. Camped 5 1/2 miles east of Athens [Ga.].

13th. Passed thrugh the town of Athens and camped 12 miles from it. We now approach the "Georgia cracker" region. "Where were you raised?" In Maine. "O. I thought you didn't belong to our sort o' people" said a very good looking woman.

14th. We encamped about 12 miles from Lawrenceville [Ga.] & as bad luck had it – near a grog shop. Put an old cracker out of camp at midnight.

15th. Passed through Lawrenceville & camped 3 miles from it.

16th. Marched 9 miles to the Chattahoochee [River] & crossed at the Warsaw ferry where I put a letter in the P.O. Marched 7 miles further. This is the Cherokee nation.

17th. Crossed the Etowah at Canton [Ga.] & camped half a mile from the river.

18th. Encamped 18 or 20 miles from N. Echotta in the gold region.

19th. ”   at New Echota. The order here for Maj. Riley is that the march be continued to Calhoun [Tenn.], the head quarters of the 4th. Inf. The marching previous to getting into the cracker region is over a bright road without shade & the sun's rays are intolerable – we then come to a narrow road lined with trees. There has been no rain on this march. We have lived on eggs & chickens. I was waiting in Canton at the Etowah for the waggons to cross & a young sister (16) of the storekeeper came in, dressed like a city schoolgirl. She was very lively like a young kitten. At length she walked out in front & (taking no notice of the number of people there) looking at a young bumpkin exclaimed, "Well John, I congratulate you on being married. I understand you are in clover up to your hatband."

Mem. (King–coach'em)[?].

20th. Lt. Shiras[38] arrived while I was in Gen. Floyd's[39] office from Calhoun – says the indians are allowed to stay till September. "I hope not in Georgia, says Floyd, for I shall march against them as soon as they appear there. Everyone who approaches will be in danger of rope or lead."

21st. Early – Marched from New Echota crossing the [Etowah] river.

22nd. Continued the march, stopped 26 miles from Calhoun at a river & bridge.

23rd. Proceeded to Calhoun (Fort Cass) & thence three miles to Fort Foster, the camp of the other six companies of the 4th.

24th. Visited Gen. Scott – an official call.

July

10th. Jewel deserted stealing 20$ from me.

25th. News of my promotion to 1st Lieut. of 7 July.

August

1st. Morgan arr[ive]d having lost all my baggage in bringing it from Baton Rouge.

9th. Detached from Camp Worth at the Rattle Snake spring to form Camp McClure.

10th. News of my reversion back to 2d Lieut.

November

6 – Camped 6 miles from Ft. Cass, 9 miles from Athens [Tenn.].

7 – Marched through Athens – camped at [?] 6 1/2 miles beyond.

8 – Camped on Corntassle branch 7 mi from Madisonville [Tenn.].

9th. Forded a river – very cold – struck thru Tenn. Col. Morgan's – camped on the Tenn. (14 m).

10th. Forded the Tenn. near Hardings – camped up in the Smokey Mountains on the turnpike. Accident in the river (12 m), Parsons.

11th. Marched 9 m. camped at McElden's farm, arrived at the soldier's grave – N[orth] C[arolina].

12th. Course along the Tenn. Passed the other soldier's grave buried whe[re] he was killed. Camped 1 1/2 m. below Welch's (16 m) on the Tenn.

13th. Remained in camp.

14th. Ordered to go up to the Smokey Mts. & follow them to Oconelufty. Marched early with D & K companies. It rains steadily. Having marched three miles & separated in 3 detachments. One up the main creek (Crisp's) & 2 on the opposite sides of the branch. Lt. Graham with the former, myself with the latter. We all agreed to camp on the main creek with Lt. Graham. My branch forking, I took the left stream & Sergt. Willard with 1/2 of K Comp. took the other. It continuing to rain hard I encamped at 4 o'clock without joining Sergt. Willard. Passed a miserable night in a constant rain.

15th. Started early for Graham's camp expecting to meet everybody there. Crossed a great mountain river & followed down a branch to the main creek at the mouth of the former[. F]ound Graham's camp fires still burning, nobody there. Found RETURNED printed on a stump. This was 12 o'c[lock]. With a variety of suppositions in my head to account for the return I made a forced march over "knob" & "gully" to Camp Scott about 12 m. off. I arrived at dark & reported my expedition impracticable in such weather. Sergt. W. arrived only 1/2 an hour before me having encamped on my own trail a mile & a half from when I did last night. Today he struck Lt. Graham's trail & finding D compy. had gone back he thought I had gone with them & took the same direction.

16th. Lay at Camp Scott – perfectly tired out.

17th. ditto.

18th. Ordered to take my camp up on a ridge of Mts. between the sources of Crisp's & Hazlenut Creeks & establish it there in such a manner as to prevent indians from passing that way to the Tennessee R. as we are now operating on the north side of that river, where the indians are supposed to be. Started early & found it heavy climbing all day – had some very extensive views & some very fine ones – saw [Ft?] Lindsey. Found a fine spring in one of the "gaps" or passing places & camped – resolved to guard this place with 1/2 my comp. & send the rest to a similar place 5 miles further. After dark I ascended the highest cheek of the gap to reconnoitre. I discovered a small light on the top of an opposite mountain – it was descending it. Perhaps it was the murderers! I called the guide – it was so dark he could not tell what Mt. it was or which way to go to it. However, with 3 guides & 6 soldiers I set out instantly – at random. In 10 minutes a dense fog was drawn over the scene & obliged us to return. A heavy mist succeeded – which turned to snow & we had a perfect winter storm all night.

19th. Sent a Sergt. & 8 [men] & a guide to take up the other position. Stormy all day.

20th. I waked or rather uncovered my head last night & found the sky as full of bright stars as I ever saw it. I went up to reconnoitre, made no discoveries. This morning I pointed out the Mt. where I saw the light & the direction in which it was proceeding to the guides. It was on the summit of the main ridge of the Smokey Mts. & descending towards Tennessee side. I took a party of 6 men & 2 guides & set out for the "Double Springs" where within 100 yds. of each other heads Little River on one side of the Smokey Mts. & Crisp's Creek on the other. This place is not far from the Mt. on which I saw the light & is an old camping place of the Indians. It is just at the edge of the Laurel Region & at the western extremity of the Balsam Region. Our course was along the ridge on which we are encamped till it brings us onto the Smokey Mts. (between 6 & 7 miles). We then turn to the right & follow that ridge about [?]. At 10 o'clock we halted at our other camp which we found as uncomfortable as our own – the wind being very keen & having a clear sweep. The land here is covered with small black timber & grass which is green all winter. A very good winter range for cattle when not as at present covered with frozen snow. Our old guide told us that he had entered a hundred acres of sugar maple land less than a mile from that spot, but was afraid he should not secure it as he had not been able "conveniently" to raise the money for it. On being asked what it amounted to he'd replied 10$. The land he added would have been but 5 cts. an acre if I had entered less than a hundred. I was surprised at the low price of rich land which is on account of its locality & no less so at the inconvenience of raising 10$ when balanced against a hundred acres. The fact is the country is thinly settled & every man works on his own farm & lives on its product. Many of the loafers about the cities & big towns who obtain their subsistence in a way that destroys their comfort in this world & forbids all idea of it in the next, might here find an honest & a proper livelihood. The husband & the wife might live without fighting. Best of all they would preserve that sweet peace of mind which once broken, taints if not destroys the whole current of a man's happiness.

Being unwell I remain at the camp & sent on the rest of the party – who took the third guide with them. They got back at 3 o'clock having met with nothing worth mentioning. Save that the travelling was so bad that the old guide gave out & was left in rear with one of his sons.

21st. Broke up the other camp at night.

22nd. Early marched for Camp Scott. Found news of my re–promotion to 1st Lieut. of 7th July.

23rd. P.M. Three of the murderers, George, Lake & Lowan[?] were shot at Camp Scott. They all bore it like philosophers – like plain matters of fact – common sense indians – [Lowan?] showed no kind of emotion – George's face shone with anxious perspiration – Lake was much troubled.

24th. At 11 A.M. marched for Calhoun.

December

12th. Left Fort Cross under orders to go to Arkansas to relieve the 7th Inf. at Ft. Gibson. Marched 14 m. had a "promenade all round."

13th. Camped at Widow M[orse]'s. 15 M. from Roy's Landing.

14th. Crossed the [T I G Y][?] at Brainerd – where there is a mill, a good large dwelling house & a school house (with a cupola). Crossed the Tennessee at Roy's Landing. "Forward and back all hands round."

15th. To Kelly's ferry. The right wing embarked on board the Harkaway, the left on board the Holston.

16th. Both the boats left Kelly's ferry for Decatur, Ala. At evening ours passed the Harkaway which was "wooding". A few miles further came to Lang Island – the boat grounded. The Harkaway took the other side of the island & we saw nor heard no more of them.

17th. It rained all day – could not get off. Heard of the Harkaway. She is aground about 6 miles below us.

18th. Landed all the men – at night she went off clear amidst the cheers of all hands & all the troops. Lay all night in deep water. Heard the Harkaway had got off.

19th. Underway again – grounded on the same place where the Harkaway did. Landed the men immediately, & as good luck would have it after trying all day she was got clear after dark.

20th. In the morning late got underway again.

21st. At night arrive at Decatur.

22nd. Transferred visitors to the rail cars & arrived at Tuscumbia [Ala.]. I was left behind but overtook them at night.

23rd. Went down in the steamboat Victoria 20 miles & was landed on the bank where we passed the night.

24th. Went over the shoals ten miles in Arks[40] to Waterloo [Tenn.] where we overtook the right wing. On the same day we embarked in the st[ea]mboa]t Melton & two Arks & commenced descending the river again.

25th. Christmas was duly noticed on board.

26th. Stopped before night at Paducah, Kentucky & lay there till 12 next day.

27th. Entered the Ohio to proceed to its mouth.

28th. Entered the Mississippi which we found to be full of ice. Descended 18 miles & turned back as it was found to be perfectly obstructed.

29th. Still going back [?] at 12 M. attained the mouth of the Ohio.

30th. Landed at Trinity & camped. The Milton left us for Paducah.

31st. Muster

28 Entered the Mississippi ~~& the~~ which was found full of ice. Descended ?? miles & turned back as it was found to be perfectly obstructed

29 Still going back & ?? at 12 M. attained the mouth of the Ohio.

30th Landed at Trinity & camped The Milton left us for Paducah.

31st Muster

Jan 1st 1839. Left Trinity alone on horseback for Jonesboro, with leave for 4 days. Passed thro "The Mounds" "America" & and. at Jonesb. at dark — It rained all day.

2. A party of Emigrating Cherokees passed thro' Town. Brown's party. It rained all day

45. Opening page of the Diary of Lt. Henry Prince for 1839

THE DIARY OF LT. HENRY PRINCE

1839

January

1st. Left Trinity alone on horseback for Jonesboro [Tenn.], with leave for 4 days – passed thru "The Mounds", "America" & arr[ive]d at Jonesb. at dark – it rained all day.

2nd. A party of Emigrating Cherokees passed thru town – Brown's party. It rained all day.

3rd. Cloudy, warm & dry overhead – very muddy or very slippery. Visited Brown's camp. Saw several of my civilized indian acquaintances. Melton returned to Trinity.

4th. Left Jonesb. at daylight, arr[ive]d. at Trinity at 3 o'clock – in time for dinner.

5th. Continuing warm – fine prospect of the gorge giving way. In the afternoon the river had fallen a foot! This looks like it.

6th. The Melton went down to the gorge. She went thro it – met a Steamboat, learn't that the ice had been gone not more than two hours, which enrapturing news she brought to us at night.

7th. Early embarked on board the Melton as before – & bid a long farewell to Trinity. Passed the wreck of a snagged steamboat.

8th. Were meeting steamboats all day. Sometimes 4 or 5 were in sight at the same time – at difft. distances passed the wrecks of three snagged steamboats.

9th. At 10 A.M. I saw the 1st Chickasaw Bluff.

10th. At Memphis. Left same day.

11th. At the mouth of the Arkansas – general impression that we cannot get up. Entered the mouth – it looks very low & full of snaggs

– sticking up in every which way – lay still all night.

12th. Some bubbles are on the water which is considered a sign that it is rising. By the marks set out it is supposed it rose an inch in the night.

13th. Arrived at the cut off & tied up – the river rose a few inches last night.

14th. Still at the "cut off". Simons died, buried him on the bank – river rose a foot & more in the last night. Steamboat with troops passed down.

15th. River continues to rise gradually. Set out again & tied up in the evening.

16th. Before we went to bed last night the river had risen three feet! and this morning when we got up it had rised 6 or 7 more!! [T]he current is now immense & full of drifting logs or rather trees, roots & all, & is covered with piles & sheets of foam. We were all day today making 6 miles! so powerful is the current. In the evening left one of our keels & all the right wings tied up to the bank & set out with the others at dusk. At 12 o'clock we are about 2 miles from them & tied up ourselves at this time. Experienced great difficulty amongst the drifting stuff – <u>waterlogged</u>. The engineer sings out "I want to work the engine". The pilot, "you can't, the wheel will get afoul of the log under her." "I must or we'll blow up as sure as hell!" So he worked it very slowly.

17th. Passed "Pine Bluff" [Ark.], a town – and got up 40 miles! But it was hard work. The river is full! to the brim!

April 5. '42 Rode from Ft Cross to
Tampa - Flirt followed me. She got very
tired & when I would ride up to a big log she
would get onto the log & jump into the saddle
when she would ride along with me & go
to sleep. It is not pleasant riding alone
in such a dreary & monotonous country.
I'll take no more such rides - A man's
left too much to his own reflections & they
too often fail to be amusing. Tampa looks
very pretty when first you come in sight of
it getting out of the woods. The new the river the
buildings the bay, Gadsdens point beyond it -
all striking. A very level & simple view but
vast & brilliant - so much water & so many
white houses. - Say canoe full of drunk
indians - some drunk sitting on the wharf. All
went away but one - he asked some boys who were
floating along to take him in - seeing he was so
drunk they would not notice him. Without saying
anything he commenced laying aside his articles
of dress - He would have thrown himself overboard
if other (sober) indians had not observed him from
on board Steam boat & baulked him while some
approached & took him in canoe

46. Opening page of the Diary of Lt. Henry Prince for 1842

THE DIARY OF LT. HENRY PRINCE

1842

April

5th. Rode from Ft. Cross[1] to Tampa – Flirt[2] followed me. She got very tired & when I would ride up to a big log she would get onto the log & jump into the saddle where she would ride along with me & go to sleep. It is not pleasant riding alone in such a dreary & monotonous country. I'll take no more such rides. A man is left too much to his own reflections & they too often fail to be amusing. Tampa looks very pretty when first you come in sight of it getting out of the woods. The river, the buildings, the bay, Gadsdens point,[3] the sea beyond it – all striking. A very level & simple view but vast & brilliant – so much water & so many white houses. [Many] canoes full of drunk indians – some drunk sitting on the wharf. All went away but one – he asked some boys who were floating along to take him in. Seeing he was so drunk they would not notice him. Without saying anything he commenced laying aside his articles of dress – he would have thrown himself overboard if other (sober) indians had not observed him from on board Steam boat & baulked him while some approached & took him in canoe.

6th. Just as all were quitting supper at Allens, Col. Worth[4] entered, Maj. Belknap[5] was with him. Spoke to Maj. B. – did not speak to Col. W. Interview with Col. Garland.[6]

7th. Ready to return to Ft. Cross in the morning. Directed to wait. Col. Worth wanted to learn something of me about the Withlacoochy, the situation of the Cove Charlo popka[Tsala Apopka][7] &c. I communicated it to Cooper[8] who wished me to write it. While writing it in

Cooper's office (I being all alone) Col. W. came in & hem[me]d a little
– I took no notice of him. Dined at Allen's & left Tampa. Was riding
pretty fast when I missed my great coat – found it in the middle of the
road two miles behind, a great turkey gobler was close by it – had no
gun. Thirteen miles from Tampa overtook some wagons, slept by them
– they gave me some fine perch – caught in the hole where they dipped
up their water.

8th. Before daylight moved on again. Twenty miles from Ft. Cross
stopped to get a pony – was riding up to catch him when to my surprise I found it was a panther. Spurred off & left him at his will – he
did not once take his eyes off of me from the moment I first saw him
till the woods intervened – but followed me turning his head & lifting
it up over the bushes & where once they got too high for him, he ran
round them. Wanted a gun, his skin would have been a treasure. At
eleven A.M. was at Ft. Cross.

10th. Left Ft. Cross with F Comp., Capt. Page & Lt. Wallen[9] both
along – camped at Lake Lindsay – very warm day – 11 ms.

11th. Marched 7 ms. to Charlo popka & 4 more to Ft. Cooper.
Tried to find the trail near Ft. Cooper leading into Charlopopka –
counldn't.

12th. Marched to within a mile of Camp Izard & camped. Capt.
Page & I took a ride out & on approaching the river at Clinch's battle
ground discovered Major Belknaps' fleet of canoes. Belknap, Mont-
gomery, Buchanan, Gates, Doane, Smith, Dr. Bridsaly. Slept on Clinches
battle ground. Had an alarm in the night created by a man screaming
murder in his sleep – he thought the indians were cutting his head off.

Belknaps camp on the opposite side of the river (Gaines' battle
ground 27th. Feb. 36) was roused also – by the sentinel who protested
he saw a squaw run along in the bushes.

13th. Started up the river – detached – joined the whole (boats &
all) at Scott's battle ground – few moccasin tracks but 2 weeks old at
least. Had a bad time wading into the Charlo popka, could not get the
pony along – a good little fellow – brave as a lion & strong – stripped
him naked & left him up to the hub in mud & roots a mile or two
inside of the cypress swamp. Long before turning the pony loose I
found every body had gone on but about a dozen men who were help-
ing me to coax the pony. We were almost lost in the swamp for an

hour not knowing which course would get us through it – at length we debouched into the open woods & found we had left the river two miles to our left or the river had left us, I do not know which. Being acquainted with the ground I took a trail by which I struck the river 4 or 5 miles off & got ahead of all the rest – sat down on the bank of the river & waited for them – took a lunch – a drink of brandy which I had saved out of the pony's pack & caught a handsome string of fish. Directly the boats came in sight rushing along & the troops on the land cracking the bushes, pulling & hauling at the vines ripping & tearing their garments & occasionally letting off a compliment to the indians in no elegant lauguage. "Sacre toneu! Dunder & blixen! By the holy St. Patrick doesn't this mind ye of the bogs at home Larry? Shut up that clattering phiz of yours & mind whose face you are snapping the bushes into. There by – ! there goes my cap. I say! Take your ramrod & catch that cap floating by there – save the pipe & tobacco! My shoe was comed off [?] [?] morass I can't know when at I shall do heh! Move on, move on. Forward men – the boats are getting out of hearing. &c &c."

Passed many orange groves in the wild hammocks but it would be difficult to prove them to be native. Got separated from the boats, climbed a tree & saw them a mile up into a pocket – made sign & they came to us & camped. Musquitoes etc. – warm, warm.

14th. Detached having with me Lt. Wallen & 30 men to go on to "Boggy Hammock"[10] all the rest went off in the boats to try & get there by water. Had a great deal of difficulty & lost much time in finding a way out from the river thro the swamp to the opening but took the trail after I got out & by a hard march reached the spot at sunset. Planted a flag on the bank for the boats to see & camped in a Hammock island – surrounded by marsh.

15th. Suffered very much all night from the muskitoes & heat – most of the men without blankets. Those that had them could not protect themselves from the musquitoes on account of the warmth – men walking about all night, smoked a pipe to make me drowsy – fell asleep & waked nearly devoured – bit all to pieces. Moved into another hammock, camped along side an extensive orange thicket – ripe oranges were gathered in bushels by the men – very sour. Caught a mare & colt that came into camp. They got away again. King, one of the soldiers, lent me a clean shirt – quite a luxury – no disparagement to a Prince to wear a King's shirt. Sent some men down to the river to fish – they came up & reported that they heard talking & supposed the boats were at the flag. Sent to see. No boats there. Must have been troops on the other side [of] the river scouring the Boggy Hammock. Sorry the men did not holler. Sent them to the river to holler – too late, they got no answer.

16th. Another awful night – men suffer much – concluded to give a grand shout at the river in the morning. If I get no response, will wait till noon & then go off for Ft. Cross. If the boats don't come by that time they won't come at all. Provisions as scarce as blankets. Wallen & myself are obliged to get pork & bread of the soldiers. We eat plenty of sour oranges but that only gives us a greater appetite. Took a dozen men – went to the river – arranged them in a ring – got in the center – gave the signal – & raised three simultaneous shouts. But it sounded too much like sand hill cranes. Told them to shout promiscuously & they made another noise. If any indian families heard it I reckon they were <u>frightened</u>! <u>No answer.</u> Returned to camp, caught a day nap – was waked at ten. "Lieutenant, the boats are at the landing." Capt. Page & the remainder of our comp. joined us. The boats returned to Maj. Belknap's camp on the Pannu sofkay[Lake Panasoffkee][11] when Col. Worth arrived & sent an order for us to wait till morning for further orders.

17th. Another stinging night & warm. Maj. Belknap sent a boat for Capt. Page & myself to visit his camp in. Had a pleasant paddle. Found the Maj. encamped near a breast work of rocks made by the negroes when they fought the Tennesseans across the creek. Took dinner, received orders for a few days more scouting & returned to our own camp & our own musquitoes.

18th. Made an early start to cross the Charlo popka – commenced wading at the very start. Caught the mare & colt again. Travelling too deep for her – she couldn't get along – left her. As well as I remember we crossed ten islands – 4 very deep saw grass plains, one large field cultivated last year, a dozen lodges in it – one island had a large camp on it, deserted 3 mo[nth]s ago I suppose – had a tremendous wade from the last island to the tall pines where we made big fat fires & rested our weary bones, just at sunset.

19th. Scouted along the Charlo popka & camped at Ft. Cooper – have nothing to eat but a single partridge – eat it & still hungry. Took a soldiers rifle & went to hunt for a dear. Had a capital shot at five all in a huddle & very near say 30 yards but the gun hung fire having been loaded ever since we left Ft. Cross – set it down to <u>my luck</u> & went back to camp to tell of it.

20th. Marched to where we expected to meet Maj. Belknap 5 miles from Camp Izard. Am hungrier than ever. [Blank] says that Maj. B. will not be here till day after tomorrow. Made a bet he'd be here by 12 o'cl[oc]k tomorrow.

21st. At 10 A.M. Maj. B. arrd. with boats on the waggons – nothing said about the wager. The boats were put into the water or rather the <u>popka</u>. Lt. Gates & 25 men, an indian guide & an interpreter & I was detached in command of them. Had a novel & pleasant scout – the lillies were as thick as stars on the water for miles in some parts. Paddled about ten miles examining islands & got back to camp at sunset. While on a large island & entering an old field, I saw a smoke rising – made a charge on it with two men (all that were near me) & found it to be an old tree broken down by lightning & set on fire by the same.

22nd & 23rd. Marched to Ft. Cross.

24th. The pony has been seen on the opposite side of the river from where we left him & was making his way leisurly towards Fort Clinch.

25th. The Pony arrived from Fort Clinch led by an Express rider. All were glad to see him.

EPILOGUE

The entries of April 1842 represent the end of Prince's service in Florida during the period of the Second Seminole War. A troubled peace would come in August, announced by Col. William Worth:on the 24th: " . . . hostilities with the Indians within this Territory have ceased."

From Florida Prince was sent to Jefferson Barracks, Missouri, where he was in garrison into 1844. In the same year he served at Grande Ecore (Camp Salubrity), Louisiana, and then on Coast Survey to June 1846. He served on recruiting service for several months until appointed Adjutant, 4th Infantry, in November. In this capacity he went with the regiment to Mexico.

It was June 1847 when Prince first saw action in his second war, beginning with the defense of a convoy at Talome and again at National Bridge. In August he took part in the battles of Contreras and Churubusco, receiving the brevet rank of Captain for "gallant and meritorious conduct." Two weeks later he was seriously wounded in the battle of Molino del Rey and immediately received a brevet promotion to Major. With the army he went on to occupy Mexico City where, on September 23, his promotion to Captain was made permanent.

Along the way Prince had acquired a magnificent horse and, while convalescing, was reluctantly approached by a fellow officer who wanted to arrange a brief loan of the animal to a young Mexican he had befriended. Newly brevetted Captain Sam Grant was afraid the young man couldn't handle the fiery animal but thought "the suspicious Spanish nature would interpret any suggestion of caution as a mere disguise of ungenerosity." Prince agreed to the loan of his horse. Grant's reluctance was well-founded; the Mexican lost control, was thrown and killed minutes after mounting.

Considering himself "nearly destroyed by a [M]exican bullet," Prince was given a sick leave of absence and sent home to Eastport for what became a three-year recuperation. The nature of his wound is not clear (though there are references in his correspondence to "my game ankle"), but it was not until December 1850 that he was sufficiently recovered to return to duty. Then, however, it was not, as he would have preferred, with his regiment, where "I should have commanded a post." Instead he was reassigned to Coast Survey duty where "only in comparison with a sick leave [was it] to my interest to be on that duty."

Among the many fellow West Point graduates that Prince had known well and served with through the Florida War as well as the Mexican was Benjamin Alvord, class of 1833. He and Alvord had maintained a correspondence when, from time to time, their paths had diverged. In December 1852 then-Captain Alvord, stationed in Oregon, wrote to ask a favor. "I take a friend's priviledge [sic] of asking your assistance in obtaining [appointment as Paymaster] if opportunity offers. You will best know how to go to work, who to speak to etc." In the light of their long and close relationship it is probable that Prince gave the assistance asked by the younger man. In any case, Alvord received promotion to major and appointment as paymaster in June 1854. Possibly this was the inspiration for Prince's own subsequent application for and acceptance of staff appointment as paymaster and promotion to full major one year later. This convergence of courses would have tragic consequences for the two men.

Meanwhile, Prince returned to duty with the Coast Survey in Florida where, during January, February, and March of 1854 he made a reconnaissance of the entire east coast from the St. John's river south to Jupiter Inlet, a distance of some two hundred and seventy miles. In February 1855, Professor A. D. Bache, Superintendent of the Coast Survey, notified Prince that he was relieved of duty with the Coast survey and expressed his appreciation of the "efficient, zealous, and thorough service which you have rendered." In reply Prince wrote that "I was bent on rendering myself efficient again, and I have been successful. I have found, too, that no medicine is more healing than the satisfaction of being useful."

As paymaster with the rank of major, Prince was sent to Washington state in 1855 and command of Fort Steilacoom on Puget Sound. Subsequently, he served on paymaster duty throughout the West: Fort Leavenworth, Kansas; Fort Kearny, Nebraska; Laramie, Dakota Territory; in Texas at Forts Lancaster and Davis and at San

Antonio; on the Utah campaign; and finally overland from Washington, D.C., to California and back. Recurring trouble with his old wounds called for a leave of absence in 1859 and another year recuperating in Eastport, not returning to duty until 1861. In July, three months into civil war, the governor of Maine, Israel Washburne, recommended to President Lincoln that Prince be made brigadier general of volunteers "because I believe him to be the best man I know for promotion." Others from Maine also appealed to the president, and, more than a year later, Gen. Pope, exiled to the midwest for the defeat at Second Bull Run, wired Stanton, "I have no one . . . to help me. Will you not appoint Major Prince Brig. Genl. for service on the frontier." Unknown to Pope, Prince had received the promotion four months earlier, had since served in the Northern Virginia Campaign and the battle of Cedar Mountain, been wounded and captured by the Confederates, not to be released until December. In absentia he was promoted to Brevet Lt. Colonel in the Regular Army for the usual "gallant and meritorius service."

Following repatriation Prince again took the field, first in North Carolina operations, then in pursuit of the Rebels after Gettysburg, being engaged in several sharp actions including the unfortunate affair of Mine Run, November 26 through December 3, 1863, in which he shared the blame for the Union failure. In 1864 and '65 he was employed primarily in garrison command in Tennessee, Alabama, and South Carolina, meanwhile receiving brevet promotion to colonel and brigadier general simultaneously.

Prince was mustered out of Volunteer service after the war, returning to paymaster duties with the regular army in Boston and New York until April 1869 when he was appointed Chief Paymaster, Department of the East. Five years later in New York City, concerned with pending legislation, he wrote a letter to an old comrade-in-arms, now President, Sam Grant, to whom he had once loaned a horse.

February 9th, 1874.

To the President.

The bill enforcing the retirement of Army officers at sixty-two years of age now before Congress will in my own case retire as efficient and utilable a servant as the government can have in the position of paymaster. I can (and am willing to) pay in Oregon, Alaska or Arizona, at Boise City or Fort Yuma, or any other place, as well as anyone. And there can be no hands in which the public funds are more secure than mine, if experience is any criterion of such security by proper care and correct disbursement.

If true economy in the household manage [sic] of the government is greatly desirable at the present epoch one instance of this kind proves the compulsory feature to be not required by the interest of the people.

Henry Prince had turned sixty-two the year before. Clearly he had a strong personal interest in this matter of retirement. Whether Grant took any hand in the matter is not known, but Prince was retained and, in the following year, transferred to the Division of the Pacific.

There was one more promotion before the end. From San Francisco on March 15, 1877, Prince acknowledged his acceptance of the permanent rank of lieutenant colonel and appointment as deputy paymaster general. His old friend, Benjamin Alvord, was paymaster general.

Beside wounds suffered in three wars, Henry Prince had long been suffering from Bright's disease, or nephritis, an acute and chronic disease of the kidneys. Brought on by exhausting work or excessive exposure to sunlight (among other things), identified only twenty years before by an English physician, Richard Bright, the disease could bring on fatigue, nausea, and swelling around the eyes, ankles, and other parts of the body. It likely would end with kidney failure and death. There was no effective treatment. Whether morbid concern for his health brought on changes in Prince's personality or whether it was the pain and distress of wounds and illness, late in 1879, Paymaster General Alvord recommended to the adjutant general that Prince be retired, being "satisfied . . . that the irritable and morbid condition of his mind is such that he cannot properly discharge the duties of his office."

The first Prince knew of this was one month later when his replacement arrived in San Francisco on December 18 and gave him a copy of Alvord's letter the same evening. "Although at first stunned at the perusal of it . . . I at once commenced preparations to repair to Washington and reply to it." His retirement was scheduled for the 31st, now only two weeks away. He crossed the continent in ten days, arriving in Washington on the 28th, carrying affidavits from medical officers testifying that "the charactor and condition of his mind . . . is not irritible or morbid." Prince wrote to the adjutant general: "I call heaven and earth to witness that nothing has ever transpired in my office or out of it, public or private, which can supply the least basis or support to the paymaster general's theory." Added to the anguish of abrupt retirement was the fact that "he was first for promotion and a vacancy [was] imminent." With only hours remaining, he arranged a personal (and surely painful) meeting with Alvord himself, submitted to him his letter to the adjutant general. To no avail. Alvord read the letter, replied: "I . . . [recommend] to you not to send it, not to make the application contained in it for a Court of Enquiry . . . I recommend this in the most friendly spirit, having had with you a life long contact, and regretting very much the duty I have felt compelled to perform."

Prince was 68, Alvord 66. Not young men. For nearly fifty years their careers had been nearly identical, from West Point through three wars to the paymaster's department. War by war, rank by rank. Both suffered from kidney disease. Alvord, having brought his friend's service to an end, would retire at his own request in six months, die in five years. For Prince a lifetime of service was over, a friendship ended. He had never married. Only retirement, illness, and old age lay ahead.

He returned to New England, living in Boston and vicinity, rarely visiting Eastport, though he sent a liberal donation to the First Congregational Society regularly every quarter, his principal communication with his old home. The years must have seemed a burden to him. His only surviving sister, Sarah Houghton, died. He had no other near relatives. Loneliness, constant pain from his wounds, chronic kidney problems, loss of hearing, and, if Alvord was correct, an already morbid state of mind, must have combined to bring despair. In 1887, though he dreaded the voyage, he went abroad seeking relief. Instead, "At Baden [Switzerland] while bathing under the constant attention of a physician the wound which I received in the battle of Molino del Ray came open . . . Finding it continually getting worse I came here [Geneva] on the 19 Oct . . . and put myself in the care of Professor Vulliet. . . . After a surgical operation today [31 Oct. 1889] the Dr. encouraged me to hope for speedy improvement."

The state of the wound may have improved, but the kidney disease did not. By early July 1892 Prince had made his way to London and taken rooms in Morley's hotel on Trafalgar Square. In addition to his other ailments he now had "a distressing attack of asthma." For some six weeks he had been attended, off and on, by Dr. Samuel Mills, surgeon. "He [Prince] was in the habit of talking about his health and about dying and asked [Mills] how long his life would last." Fearful that his kidney disease would go to his brain, leaving him an imbecile, "he even went so far as to ask . . . whether [Mills] could not give him something to send him to sleep so that he would not wake again. He said he was so old and suffered such great pain that it would be a great kindness if [Mills] would put him out of it."

Prince made his will, paid his bills, sent his surplus money back to Eastport, arranged for the cremation of his body, and deposited money with friends to cover his funeral expenses. On Wednesday, August 17, he visited the gunshop of Cogswell and Harrison at 226, the Strand, only a few blocks from his hotel. He explained to the salesman, George Russell, that he wanted to purchase a revolver "for self protection." On Friday he returned, said he "could not get the weapon to act." Russell put it right for him.

In his room that evening, letters written, the taste of beef tea on his lips, the old man ended his suffering the only way he could. Nearly sixty years before in Florida he had written: "What is it to die . . . to be shot in some vital part and suffer no more!"

NOTES

Introduction

1 Prince to Secretary of War, 12 January 1831; Jonathan D.Weston, *History of Eastport and Vicinity* (Boston: Marsh, Capen & Lyon, 1834) 46.

2 Harold A. Davis, *An International Community on the St. Croix* (Orono, Maine: University of Maine at Orono, 1974) 95–114; C. Donald Brown, "Eastport: A Maritime History," *The American Neptune Journal* XXVIII, 2 (1968) 4–7; *The Eastport Sentinel* 31 Aug. 1892.

3 Davis 50; Weston 49.

4 Davis 116–17; Weston 45, 56–7.

5 Weston 57–8.

6 Davis 101.

7 Ibid.

8 Brown 8; Weston 51; James Ripley to Secretary of War, 12 Jan. 1831; Ezekiel Holmes to Secretary of War, 13 Jan. 1831.

9 Ripley.

10 George Washington Cullum, *Register of Graduates and Former Cadets United States Military Academy* (West Point: The West Point Alumni Foundation Inc., 1960) 171; *The Centennial of the United States Military Academy as West Point, New York, 1802–1902,* Vol. I (Washington, D.C.: U.S. Government Printing Office, 1904) 229.

1836

1 Settlement on the St. Johns River eighteen miles west of St. Augustine.

2 1st. Lt. Francis Littleberry Dancy; See Francis B. Heitman, *Historical Register and Dictionary of the United States Army,* Vol. I. (Washington, D.C.:U.S. Government Printing Office, 1903), 362; Cullum, 179.

3 "Who goes there?"

4 First inland town established by whites in Florida (1820), twenty-five miles NW of Fort King (present-day Ocala). Still in existence.

5 Auld Lang Syne was a sugarcane plantation built by Bvt. Brig. Gen. Duncan Lamont Clinch on a 400-acre tract purchased in 1823. "Picketification" was the construction of a log palisade around a portion

of the area for protection of troops, erected in December 1835 under the direction of Lt. Gustavus S. Drane, afterword referred to as "Ft. Drane."

6 Bvt. 2nd Lt. John Graham, 4th Inf; Heitman, 468; Cullum '60, 186.

7 Bvt. Major Francis Langhorne Dade and his command of 107 officers and men were attacked by Seminoles on 28 December 1835. After a day-long battle only two soldiers survived to return to Fort Brooke; Frank Laumer, *Massacre!* (Gainesville, Fla.: University of Florida Press, 1968); Laumer, *Dade's Last Command* (Gainesville, Fla.: University Press of Florida, 1995).

8 Tampa, now the major city on Tampa Bay, was at this time a small community that was gathering around Fort Brooke, established in 1824.

9 Fort King, 100 miles north of Fort Brooke, had been established in 1827 within the present limits of the city of Ocala; Eloise Robinson Ott & Louis Hickman Chazel, *Ocali Country, Kingdom of the Sun* (Ocala, Fla.: Marion Publishers, 1966), 23-25.

10 Lt. Col. David Emanuel Twiggs; Heitman, 976.

11 An officer of volunteers.

12 A colonel of volunteers.

13 Maj. Gen. Richard Keith Call; Heitman, 274; Herbert J. Doherty Jr., *Richard Keith Call Southern Unionist* (Gainesville, Fla.: University of Florida Press, 1961).

14 2nd Lt. William Elon Basinger; Heitman, 197; Cullum '60, 182. 2nd Lt. Robert Rich Mudge; Heitman, 734; Cullum '60, 185. Both killed with Dade.

15 Bvt. 2nd Lt. Richard Henderson; Heitman, 522; Cullum, 187. Class-mate of Prince at West Point, killed with Dade.

16 Believed to be 2nd Lt. Charles Jarvis Whiting; Heitman, 1029; Cullum '60, 186. Classmate of Prince at West Point.

17 Then Brig. Gen. Winfield Scott; Heitman, 870.

18 Prince spells this variously Ouith, Ouithlaetc, Ouithla, Ouith&c, etc. On the battle, see John Bemrose, *Reminiscences of the Second Seminole War*, ed. John K. Mahon (Gainesville, Fla.: University of Florida Press, 1966), 48-53; Rembert W. Patrick, *Aristocrat In Uniform: General Duncan L. Clinch* (Gainesville, Fla.: University of Florida Press, 1963), 93-111; John K. Mahon, *History of the Second Seminole War, 1835—1842* (Gainesville, Fla.: University Presses of Florida, 1967), 108-112; Frank Laumer, "Encounter At The River," *Florida Historical Quarterly* 46 (1967): 322-29.

19 Osceola, called Powel by many whites, after the man believed to be his father. See Patricia R. Wickman, *Osceola's Legacy* (Tuscaloosa, Ala.: University of Alabama Press, 1991).

20 Bvt. Maj. Gen. Edmund Pendleton Gaines. See Heitman, 442; James W. Silver, *Edmund Pendleton Gaines Frontier General* (Baton Rouge, La.: Louisiana State University Press, 1949).

21 Capt. Gustavus S. Drane; Heitman, 382.

22 Assumed to be a playful reference to the French "*flot*," referring to bodies of water; specifically "flottard" Naval cadet; baggy trousers, *Cassell's French-English English-French Dictionary*, ed. Ernest A. Baker (New York: Funk & Wagnalls, 1951), 346.

23 Gen. (Georgia Militia) Wiley Thompson, agent for the Seminoles since 1833, killed by Osceola on 28 December 1835.

24 1st Lt. Constantine Smith; Heitman, 895.

25 Erastus Rogers, sutler at Fort King.

26 Accepted spelling is *Cudjo*, a Negro interpreter.

27 2nd Lt. Roswell Walter Lee; Heitman 625; Cullum '60, 185.

28 Either Richmond or Georgia Blues, volunteer units.

29 Presumed to be Capt. Charles Mynn Thruston; Heitman, 960; Cullum '60, 173.

30 Bvt. Brig. Gen. Duncan Lamont Clinch was in command of all troops in Florida; Heitman, 310.

31 A port city on the Gulf of Mexico 40 Miles south of Tallahassee.

32 Lt. Col. William Sewell Foster, though according to Heitman, 432, still a major at this date.

33 2nd Lt. Henry Lee Scott; Heitman, 868; Cullum '60, 185.

34 Believed to be Bvt. 2nd Lt. Alexander M. Mitchell; Heitman 715; Cullum '60, 187.

35 2nd Lt. Benjamin Alvord; Heitman, 161; Cullum '60, 185.

36 Believed to be 2nd Lt. Abraham C. Myers; Heitman, 739; Cullum '60, 185.

37 Bvt. 2nd Lt. Isaac Van Duzer Reeve; Heitman, 822; Cullum '60, 187.

38 This branch of the Withlacoochee River is 7 1/2 miles north of the Big Withlacoochee by the Fort King Road.

39 Captain Upton Sinclair Fraser; Heitman, 434.

40 Bvt. 2nd Lt. John Low Keais; Heitman, 586; Cullum '60, 187.

41 Asst. Surgeon John Slade Gatlin; Heitman, 450. For further information on Gatlin and other medical officers of the period see E. Ashby Hammond, *The Medical Profession in 19th Century Florida, A Biographi-*

cal Register (Gainesville, Fla.: University of Florida Press, 1996).

42 Capt. George Washington Gardiner; Heitman, 445; Cullum '60, 172.

43 Name given to Clinch's plantation after being fortified under the direction of Capt. Gustavus Drane.

44 Believed to be 1st Lt. Timothy Paige; Heitman, 765; Cullum '60, 178.

45 A firing of guns in token of joy.

46 Believed to refer to Capt. Armstrong of the schooner *Motto*, the ship which had brought Dade and his company up from Key West to Fort Brooke.

47 2nd Lt. Thomas Beasly Linnard; Heitman, 634; Cullum '60, 183.

48 The burning of the priming in the pan of a flintlock musket without discharging the piece.

49 These partial uniforms were likely taken from the dead of Dade's command. This attack by Indians dressed as soldiers was extremely unusual, if not unique, and clearly successful in causing confusion among the soldiers.

50 Camp/Fort Izard, barricade and blockhouse built during this action, named for 1st Lt. James Farley Izard, wounded here 28 February 1836, died 5 March 1836; Heitman, 566; Cullum, 181. This site is now managed by the Seminole Wars Historic Foundation under a special use agreement with the Southwest Florida Water Management District.

51 Presumably the heart of dead pine trees, pitch-filled, commonly used for fires, then and now.

52 2nd Lt. James Duncan; Heitman, 387; Cullum '60, 186.

53 From Seminole *"estechatti"* for "Indian"; William H. Simmons, *Notices of East Florida with An Account of the Seminole Nation of Indians by a Recent Traveler in the Province* (Charleston, S.C.: Privately printed by A. E. Miller, 1822), 98;" "Iste-chati," W. W. Smith, *Sketch of the Seminole War, and Sketches During A Campaign* (Charleston, S.C.: Dan J. Dowling, 1836), 93.

54 Believed to be 2nd Lt. John Eaton Henderson; Heitman, 522; Cullum '70, 224.

55 According to Heitman, 209, Francis Smith Belton was captain at this time, though previously holding the rank of major.

56 A quick glance.

57 Persifor Frazer Smith, appointed colonel of Louisiana volunteers only a month before, commanded the Louisiana Volunteers; later brigadier general of regulars (1856); Heitman, 902.

58 Captain Ethan Allen Hitchcock; Heitman, 532; Cullum '60, 174.

59 Jumper (Ote Emathla), Seminole leader; Mahon, 127.

60 Alligator (Halpatter Tustenuggee), Seminole leader; Mahon, 127.

61 Presumably a slang reference to bivouac. See Webster 1857, "booby-hut," "booby-hatch," 136.

62 Abraham was an interpreter as well as advisor to Micanopy.

63 Seminoles who lived in the Pease (Peas) Creek area.

64 Area around the Wacasassa River in northern Florida which reaches the Gulf between Cedar Key and Yankeetown.

65 Thought to be 2nd Lt. George Wilson; Heitman, 1046; Cullum '60, 183.

66 Believed to be Col. William Lindsay; Heitman, 634.

67 Primus, a Seminole Negro and, after capture, interpreter for whites.

68 "Holy-wockerche," Prince's translation of the Seminole "*hulwak-stchay,*" meaning "it is not good"; Smith, 103.

69 Gen. Scott, overall commander of troops in Florida at this time, had organized all troops into three main columns—Right, Left, and Center—whose goal was to converge on the Cove of the Withlacoochee, a Seminole stronghold.

70 Robert Burns, *Scots Wha Hae.*

71 Location unknown.

72 William Montrose Graham; according to Heitman, 468, Graham was promoted to major 31 December 1835; Cullum '60, 174.

73 Lt. Col. James Bankhead; Heitman, 189.

74 Maj. Richard Augustus Zantzinger; Heitman, 1068.

75 "The Complaint: or Night Thoughts" by Edward Young (1683—1765), philosophical poem first published in 1742; Magill, 22-23.

76 Bvt. Maj. William W. Lear; Heitman, 621.

77 Believed to be 1st Lt. John Breckinridge Grayson; Heitman, 479; Cullum '60, 180.

78 1st Lt. Thomas Boylston Adams; Heitman, 153; Cullum '60, 181.

79 2nd Lt. James McCready Morgan; Heitman, 725; Cullum '60, 187.

80 Dr. and Volunteer Lt. Col. Thomas Lawson, later Surgeon General of the U.S.; Heitman, 619.

81 Bvt. Maj. Henry Wilson; Heitman, 1046.

82 1st Lt. (3 days previous) Robert Christie Buchanan; Heitman, 258; Cullum '60, 183.

83 Believed to be 1st Lt. Richard B. Screven; Heitman, 870; Cullum '60, 182.

84 Capt. Clifton Wharton; Heitman, 1022.

85 Picus; in Latin legend, a brave warrior.

86 Brig. Gen. Abram Eustis; Heitman, 408.

87 Goffer (gopher), a burrowing land tortoise, a turtle.

88 Partmon Houghton, husband of Prince's sister Sophia (Sarah).

89 Abba was the second sister of Prince.

90 Maj. Mark Anthony Cooper, commanding the Georgia volunteers, for whom Fort Cooper was named.

91 Chocachatti, a center established in 1767 by a band of Upper Creek Indians northeast of Tampa in present-day Hernando County.

92 Fort Brooke, named for Col. George Mercer Brooke, established in 1824 near the southeast junction of the Hillsborough River and Tampa Bay; James W. Covington, "The Establishment of Ft. Brooke," *Florida Historical Quarterly* 31 (April 1953): 173-78; "Life At Ft. Brooke, 1824-1836," *Florida Historical Quarterly* 36 (April 1958): 319-30; "The Final Years of Ft. Brooke," *Sunland Tribune* 7 (November 1981): 41-42.

93 Believed to be Bvt. Maj. Richard Martin Sands; Heitman, 859.

94 Believed to be 2nd Lt. Francis Day Newcomb; Heitman, 744; Cullum '60, 178.

95 Possibly Asst. Surg. Adam Neill McLaren; Heitman, 674.

96 Gen. Powel here apparently refers to Osceola.

97 Federal Road, also the Fort King Road, a 100-mile road connecting Fort Brooke (Tampa) and Fort King (now Ocala). See William M. Goza, "The Ft. King Road —1963," *Florida Historical Quarterly* 43 (July 1964): 52-70.

98 Camp Foster, a temporary camp, not the stockaded fort of the same name to be built in 1837 at the intersection of the Fort King Road and the Big Hillsborough River.

99 This site would later be the location of Fort Foster.

100 The destruction of Fort Alabama is further described in Mahon, *History*, 160-61.

101 Asst. Surg. Benjamin Franklin Nourse; Heitman, 753.

102 Military pit. In this case, a moat-like ditch around the Fort studded with sharpened poles.

103 1st. Lt. John C. Casey; Heitman, 289.

104 Bvt. 2nd Lt. Stephen Theodore Tibbatts; Heitman, 960; Cullum '60, 187.

105 Believed to be 2nd Lt. George Washington Ward; Heitman, 1001; Cullum '60, 184.

106 Asst. Surg. John Meck Cuyler; Heitman, 350

107 Perhaps 2nd Lt. George Watson; Heitman, 1009; Cullum '60, 184.

108 William Bunce, entrepreneur and sea captain. See Janet Snyder Mathews, *Edge of Wilderness, A Settlement History of Manatee River in Sarasota Bay 1528—1885* (Sarasota, Fl.:Coastal Press, 1983), 74—5.

109 Judge Augustus Steele.

110 The Rancho was a commercial fishing camp below Tampa at the mouth of the Manatee River operated by William Bunce. See Mathews, 74.

111 Bvt. Maj. James McMillan Glassell; Heitman, 459.

112 A resident of Bangor, Maine.

113 Asst. Surg. John C. Reynolds; Heitman, 825.

114 Maj. William Gates; Heitman, 449; Cullum '60, 120.

115 Believed to be 1st Lt. Samuel Mackenzie; Heitman, 672; Cullum '60, 184.

116 Believed to be 1st Lt. David Hammond Vinton; Heitman, 988; Cullum '60, 177.

117 Believed to be Maj. Daniel Randall; Heitman, 814.

118 Prince was promoted from Bvt. 2nd Lt. to 2nd Lt. 11 June 1836; Heitman, 807.

119 Maj. John Mountfort; Heitman, 733.

120 Believed to be 2nd Lt. Samuel Moses Plummer; Heitman, 795; Cullum '60, 187.

121 Believed to be 2nd Lt. William Henry De Forest; Heitman, 364; Cullum '60, 187.

122 Col. John F. Lane; Heitman, 614; Cullum '60, 181, in command of Creek volunteers.

123 2nd Lt. Joseph Roberts; Heitman, 835; Cullum '60, 186.

124 Maj. Benjamin Kendrick Pierce; Heitman, 791.

125 "Lock the door behind us" (colloquial).

126 Maj. Gen. Thomas Sidney Jesup; Heitman, 573. See Chester L. Kieffer, *Maligned General, The Biography of Thomas Sidney Jesup* (San Rafael, California: Presidio Press, 1979).

127 Maj. Sylvester Churchill; Heitman, 301.

128 Believed to be 2nd Lt. John Addison Thomas; Heitman, 954; Cullum '60, 185.

129 Believed to be 2nd Lt. John Wolcott Phelps; Heitman, 788; Cullum '60, 188.

130 2nd Lt. William Brickett Arvin; Heitman, 173; Cullum '60, 188.

131 2nd Lt. Charles Belding Daniels; Heitman, 353; Cullum '60, 188.

132 Col. Archibald Henderson, Commandant of the Marine Corps.

133 Believed to be 1st Lt. John P. Davis; Heitman, 359; Cullum '60, 182.

134 Believed to be Capt. Elijah Lyon; Heitman, 649.

135 Believed to be Bvt. Maj. William L. McClintock; Heitman, 657.

136 Asst. Surg. Samuel Forry; Heitman, 429.

137 Believed to be Bvt. Lt. Col. Henry Stanton; Heitman, 916.

138 Believed to be Capt. George W. Allen; Heitman, 158.

139 Believed to be Capt. Pitcairn Morrison; Heitman, 729.

140 Believed to be Capt. Lorenzo Thomas; Heitman, 954; Cullum '60, 177.

141 See note 135 above.

142 Creek and lake, presently spelled "Thonotosassa," lying about seven miles northeast of Tampa.

143 This fort was designed by Prince and would be named Fort Foster. A full- scale replica of the fort now stands on the site.

144 Fort Armstrong, built only days before this entry, stood 1/4 mile northwest of Dade's battleground, 45 miles north of Fort Foster.

145 Camps Eustis and Birch were previous temporary camps apparently located at the intersection of the Fort King Road and the Withlacoochee, the site designated for Fort Dade.

146 1st Lt. John Fitzgerald Lee; Heitman, 625; Cullum '60, 186.

1837

1 Jim Boy, head-chief of Creek Indians.

2 Bvt. Maj. James Duncan Graham; Heitman, 468; Cullum, 174.

2 Lt. Leib, probably a volunteer officer, though no record found.

4 Fort Dade was located in the southeast quadrant of the intersection of the Fort King Road and the Withlacoochee River; Frank Laumer, "The Fort Dade Site," *Florida Anthropologist* 16 (June 1963): 33–42; Laumer, "This Was Fort Dade," *Florida Historical Quarterly* 45 (July 1966): 1–11. The site is now owned by the Seminole Wars Historic Foundation Inc.

5 Bvt. 1st Lt. Alfred Herbert; Heitman 525; Cullum 1960, 186.

6 Thought to be Bvt. Maj. Joseph S. Nelson; Heitman 743.

7 Believed to be 1st Lt. Frederick Searle; Heitman, 871;Cullum 1960, 177.

8 Coontie root (*Zamia integrifolia*), prepared by pounding in order to break down the fiber and force out the poisonous juice, then ground into flour and made into bread; Mahon, *History*, 36.

9 Wahoo Swamp, stronghold of the Seminoles, a vast area along the Withlacoochee River a few miles northwest of Dade's battleground, subject to frequent flooding.

10 Fort Clinch was built near the mouth of the Withlacoochee River.

11 Eui-faw, presumably Eufaula, originally a band of Upper Creeks who had settled northeast of Tampa Bay.

12 Black Dirt (Fuche Luste Hadjo), a Seminole chief.

13 A portion of the members of the (Upper) Creek Confederation who used red sticks as their symbol of war; Mahon, *History*, 6.

14 Not to be confused with <u>Fort</u> Foster, 22 1/2 miles northeast of Tampa, also on the Hillsborough River.

15 Probably refers to Camp Chastilion, just mentioned.

16 A tailor's smoothing iron, so called from its handle, which resembles the neck of a goose.

17 Believed to be 1st Lt. John Locke Hooper; Heitman, 540; Cullum '60, 185.

18 1st Lt. Edwin Rose; Heitman, 845; Cullum '60, 183.

19 Believed to be Bvt. 1st. Lt. James A. Chambers; Heitman, 294; Cullum '60, 175.

20 Believed to be 1st Lt. John Mackay; Heitman, 670; Cullum '60, 182.

21 Bvt. Brig. Gen Walker K. Armistead; Heitman, 169; Cullum '60, 170.

22 *Front de boeuf*, meaning "front" or "head" of beef.

23 Maj. David Moniac, Creek Mounted Volunteers; Heitman, 719; Cullum '60, 177. Moniac was a Creek Indian, graduate of West Point.

[24] 2nd Lt. William Mock; Heitman, 718; Cullum '60, 188.

[25] Believed to be 2nd Lt. Charles Bostwick Sing; Heitman, 889; Cullum '60, 188.

[26] Believed to be 1st Lt. William Phillips Bainbridge; Heitman, 182; Cullum, 178.

[27] Presumed to be Emathlochee, a Seminole chief.

[28] Believed to be Capt. John Page; Heitman, 765.

[29] Believed to be 2nd Lt. Thomas Lee Brent; Heitman, 242; Cullum '60, 187.

[30] Believed to be 1st Lt. Alexander Hamilton Bowman; Heitman, 234; Cullum '60, 179.

[31] Cloud (Yaholoochee), Seminole chief.

[32] Coa Hadjo, a leading Seminole chief.

[33] Possibly Asst. Surg. Eugene Hilarian Abadie; Heitman, 149.

[34] Camlet, a blanket made of camel hair.

[35] See Brent Richards Weisman, *Like Beads On A String, A Culture History of the Seminole Indians in Northern Peninsular Florida* (Tuscaloosa, Ala.: University of Alabama Press, 1989) 131–46.

[36] Believed to be Asst. Surg. Bernard Myles Byrne; Heitman, 271.

[37] Egmont Key, located at the mouth of Tampa Bay.

[38] Behold the sign, or badge.

[39] Governor of Cuba.

[40] Possible "to gamble."

[41] Thought to be George E. Weaver.

[42] Reference to descriptions of wild scenery typical of James Macpherson's *The Poems of Ossian.*

[43] "Boots" (servant).

[44] Believed to be Maj. Charles Mapes, paymaster; Heitman, 688.

[45] Maj. James Harvey Hook; Heitman, 540.

1838

[1] Fort Fraser, 40 miles east of Fort Brooke, named for Capt. Upton S. Fraser, killed with Dade.

[2] Fort Gardiner, named for Capt. George W. Gardiner, killed with Dade. Located 65 miles east of Fort Brooke.

3 <u>William</u> Davenport (not Taylor); Heitman, 355

4 Bvt. Maj. Gustavus Loomis; Heitman, 641; Cullum '60, 172.

5 Believed to be Capt. William Day; Heitman, 362.

6 Believed to be Capt. Joseph Pannel Taylor; Heitman, 947.

7 Believed to be Capt. Thomas Page Gwynne; Heitman, 485; Cullum '60, 174 (admitted as a West Point cadet in 1813, did not graduate with his class in 1818).

8 Col. Zachary Taylor. See Oliver Otis Howard, *General Taylor* (New York: D. Appleton and Company, 1892); Holman Hamilton, *Zachary Taylor Soldier of the Republic* (Indianapolis, Ind.: Bobbs-Merrill, 1941); Heitman, 949.

9 Fort Basinger, 100 miles east and south of Fort Brooke, 25 miles south of Lake Kissimee, named for 2nd Lt. William E. Basinger, killed with Dade.

10 Maj. Benjamin Franklin Larned; Heitman, 616.

11 Fort Deynaud, 100 miles south southeast of Fort Brooke on the south bank of the Caloosahatchee River.

12 1st Lt. John W. McCrabb; Heitman, 660; Cullum '60, 185.

13 Believed to be 1st Lt. James Madison Hill; Heitman, 530; Cullum '60, 183.

14 Believed to be 2nd Lt. William Gain Grandin; Heitman, 469; Cullum '60, 189.

15 Maj. Bennet Riley; Heitman, 831.

16 Battle of Lake Okeechobee, 25 December 1837; see Mahon, *History*, 227-31.

17 Holate-chee (possibly Holatoochee, brother or cousin of Micanopy; see Mahon, *History*, 127.

18 Believed to be 2nd Lt. Marcus Claudius Marcellus Hammond; Heitman, 495; Cullum '60, 188.

19 1st Lt. Robert Anderson; Heitman, 164; Cullum '60, 179; would command Fort Sumter during first battle of the Civil War.

20 Believed to be Lt. Osborn Cross; Heitman, 341; Cullum '60, 179.

21 Believed to be 1st Lt. William Phillips Bainbridge; Heitman, 183; Cullum '60, 178.

22 Lt. Col. Alexander Ramsay Thompson; Heitman, 955; Cullum '60, 172.

23 Believed to be 1st Lt. Edwin Burr Babbitt; Heitman, 177; Cullum '60, 180.

24 Believed to be 2nd Lt. James Hughes Stokes; Heitman, 928; Cullum '60, 187.

25 Sam Jones (Arpeika), Mikasuki chief; see Mahon, *History*, 127-28.

26 Col. John Warren, Commander of the Florida Cavalry.

27 Santaffee (Santa Fe) River.

28 Fort Harlee was 45 miles north and east of Fort King on the Sante Fe River.

29 Believed to be Capt. William Ward Tomkins; Heitman, 965.

30 Possibly 2nd Lt. Thomas Williams; Heitman, 1042.

31 Asst. Surg. Samuel Forry; Heitman, 429.

32 Believed to be 1st Lt. William Wall; Heitman, 997; Cullum '60, 184.

33 Possibly 2nd Lt. John H. P. O'Neale; Heitman, 759.

34 Believed to be Asst. Surg. George Rogers Clarke; Heitman, 307.

35 Site of the first military action of the 2nd Seminole War, 18 December 1835, also called the Battle of Black Point; see Mahon, *History*, 101-102.

36 Capt. Henry Waller Fowler; Heitman, 433.

37 2nd Lt. Joshua Hall Bates; Heitman, 199; Cullum '60, 189.

38 1st Lt. Alexander Eakin Shiras; Heitman, 884; Cullum '60, 185.

39 Gen. John Floyd, commanding Georgia Volunteers.

40 Ark, a large flatboat.

1842

1 Fort Cross was some 45 miles due north of Fort Brooke, northwest of Fort Dade, presumably named for Maj. Trueman Cross; Heitman, 341.

2 Prince's dog.

3 Gadsden's Point, southern tip of land that projects into Tampa Bay from the north, west, and south of Fort Brooke.

4 Col. William Jenkins Worth, commander of troops in Florida; Heitman, 1061; See Mahon, *History*, 295–320.

5 Lt. Col. William Goldsmith Belknap; Heitman, 207.

6 Col. John Garland; Heitman, 447.

7 Now spelled Tsala Apopka, a lake west of the Withlacoochee in the "Cove of the Withlacoochee," a stronghold of the Seminoles.

8 Possibly Bvt. Maj. Samuel Cooper; Heitman, 326; Cullum '60, 173.

9 Believed to be 2nd Lt. Henry Davies Wallen; Heitman, 999; Cullum '60, 191.

10 Hammock or hummock, a tract of land elevated above an adjacent marsh. Boggy Hammock is now called Kettle Island; see Weisman, 103, 105, 128, 174.

11 Lake Panasoffkee, west of the Withlacoochee, south of Lake Tsala Apopka.

BIBLIOGRAPHY

1. Books

Bemrose, John. *Reminiscences of the Second Seminole War.* Edited by John K. Mahon. Gainesville: University of Florida Press, 1966.

Covington, James W. *The Seminoles of Florida.* Gainesville: University Press of Florida, 1993.

Cullum, George Washington. *Register of Graduates and Former Cadets of the United States Military Academy . . . 1802-1960.* Boston: Westpoint Alumni Foundation, Inc., 1960.

Davis, Harold A. *An International Community of the St.Croix (1604-1930).* Orono: University of Maine, 1974.

Doherty, Herbert J., Jr. *Richard Keith Call: Southern Unionist.* Gainesville: University of Florida Press, 1961.

Hamilton, Holman. *Zachary Taylor: Soldier of the Republic.* Indianapolis: Bobbs-Merrill, 1941.

Hammond, E. Ashby. *The Medical Profession in 19th Century Florida: A Biographical Register.* Gainesville: University of Florida, 1996.

Heitman, Francis B. *Historical Register and Dictionary of the United States Army, From its Organization, September 29, 1789, to March 2, 1903.* Urbana: University of Illinois Press, 1965.

Howard, Oliver Otis. *Great Commanders: General Taylor.* New Y o r k : D. Appleton and Company, 1892.

Kieffer, Chester L. *Maligned General: A Biography of Thomas S .Jesup.* San Rafael: Presidio Press, 1979.

Kilby, William Henry. *Eastport and Passamaquoddy; A Collection of Historical and Biographical Sketches.* Eastport: E. E. Shead and Company, 1888.

Laumer, Frank. *Massacre!* Gainesville: University of Florida Press, 1968.

———. *Dade's Last Command.* Gainesville: University Press of Florida, 1995.

Mahon, John K. *History of the Second Seminole War 1835-1842.* Gainesville: University of Florida Press, 1967.

Matthews, Janet Snyder. *Edge of Wilderness, A Settlement History of Manatee River and Sarasota Bay 1528-1885.* Sarasota: Coastal Press, 1983.

Ott, Eloise Robinson and Chazal, Louis Hickman. *Ocali Country Kingdom of the Sun, A History of Marion County, Florida.* Ocala: Perry Printing Company, 1966.

Patrick, Rembert W. *Aristocrat in Uniform General Duncan L. Clinch.* Gaines-ville: University of Florida Press, 1963.

Record of Officers and Soldiers Killed In Battle and Died In Service during the Florida War. Washington, D.C.: Government Printing Office, 1882.

Silver, James W. *Edmund Pendleton Gaines Frontier General.* Louisiana: Louisiana State University Press, 1949.

Simmons, William H. *Notices of East Florida with An Account of the Seminole Nation of Indians by a Recent Traveler in the Province.* Charleston, S.C.: Privately printed by A. E. Miller, 1822.

Smith, W. *Sketch of the Seminole War.* Charleston, S.C.: Dan J. Dowling, 1936.

The Centennial of the United States Military Academy at West Point, New York . . . 1802-1902, Volume I: Addresses and Histories. Washington, D.C.: Government Printing Office, 1904.

Weisman, Brent Richards. *Like Beads on a String.* Tuscaloosa, Ala.: University of Alabama Press, 1989.

Weston, Jonathan D., Esq. *The History of Eastport and Vicinity: A Lecture Delivered April, 1834, Before the Eastport Lyceum.* Boston: Marsh, Capen and Lyon, 1834.

Wickman, Patricia R. *Osceola's Legacy.* Tuscaloosa, Ala.: University of Alabama Press, 1991.

2. Articles

Brown, C. Donald. "Eastport: A Maritime History." *American Neptune*, 1968.

Covington, James W., "The Establishment of Ft. Brooke." *Florida Historical Quarterly* 31 (April 1953) 173-78.

————. "Life at Ft. Brooke, 1824-1836." *Florida Historical Quarterly* 36 (April 1958) 319-30.

————. "The Final Years of Ft. Brooke." *Sunland Tribune* 7 (November 1981) 41-42.

Goza, William M. "The Ft. King 63." *Florida Historical Quarterly* 43 (July 1964) 52-70.

Laumer, Frank. "Encounter At The River." *Florida Historical Quarterly* 46 (April 1968) 322-329.

————. "The Fort Dade Site." *The Florida Anthropologist* (June 1963) 33-42.

————. "This Was Fort Dade." *Florida Historical Quarterly* 45 (July 1966) 1-11.

3. Newspapers

Daily Chronicle [London], 1892.

Daily News [London], 1892.

Daily Telegraph [London], 1892.

Eastport Sentinel [Maine], 1892.

Morning Post [London], 1892.

INDEX